BENEATH THE WINDOW
Early Ranch Life in the Big Bend Country

PATRICIA WILSON CLOTHIER AT AGE FOURTEEN.

BENEATH THE
WINDOW

Early Ranch Life in the Big Bend Country

BY

PATRICIA WILSON CLOTHIER

IRON MOUNTAIN PRESS
Houston, Texas
2013

Third Printing
February 2013

First Printing
November 2003

ISBN 0-9745048-1-5 (hardback)

ISBN 0-9745048-2-3 (trade paper)

Cover Design by Digital Tractor Design, Bastrop, Texas.

All photography courtesy the Wilson and Neil families.

Printed in the United States.

Published by:

IRON MOUNTAIN PRESS
Houston, Texas
www.ironmtnpress.com

In loving memory of my parents, Bergine and Homer M. Wilson Sr., and my brother, Homer M. Wilson Jr., with our pioneer neighbors, Nena and Sam Nail, and the other friends who lived in Big Bend in the 1930s and 1940s.

TABLE OF CONTENTS

ACKNOWLEDGEMENTS

Many persons have encouraged me to write about life in Big Bend. Foremost was my mother, Bergine Wilson, who spent hours with me taping the stories she remembered, hoping I might write of our life in the Chisos. After her death in 1991, I had my father's letters and ranch papers to confirm details in my memories. Julia Nail Moss and I reminisced, taped our talks, and corresponded about ranch life, our neighbors, and early history of Big Bend. Julia's support and inspiration made this book possible. Lita Brown Severin and I laughed and visited about the Code of the West. She encouraged me to finish the manuscript just days before her untimely death. Jean Bradfisch prompted me many times to persevere with my writing and finish the book. Before my brother Homer Junior's death in 1992, he told me, "Tell the real story of life on our ranch in Big Bend, Patricia."

Others contributed to this effort by sharing their memories in taped interviews, conversations, and correspondence. These included Evelyn Burnam Fulcher, Ruth

Todd McIver, Elinor Cartledge Howie, Minnie Mae Cartledge Everidge, Robert L. Cartledge II, Lucy Hannold Brubaker, Una May Wedin Narowetz, Robert Eaves, Fred Dumas, Ruby June Burcham, Apache Adams, James Owens, Anale Wilson Hodge, Jack Ward, Bill Ward, Merily and Tom Keller, and Jerry Cunningham.

My thanks go to Jean Ewald for letting me quote the Fred Rice material, Nancy Bowers, who allowed me to use information about her father, and Bob Graham of the Calvert School for his interest and for sharing pages from the 1936 school catalog. Special thanks go to Maril Crabtree for permission to use the poem "Invictus Revealed," and Kitty McCord Mendenhall for permission to use an excerpt from her poem "Brothers." I also appreciate the encouragement of Jack Skiles who wrote the foreword for this book.

Kay N. Miles and Reva Griffith read early manuscript attempts. Jack Lamkin helped with suggestions on manuscript content. Editors Susan Malone and Kyle Kovel followed with inspiration and guidance on the final writings.

Finally, I wish to acknowledge my children and grandchildren for their interest in this project. My husband, Grant, made this book possible with his patience, by listening as I worried about ways to express my stories, by reading my rewrites, and by commenting in a positive way so I had the courage to finish these stories.

Foreword

The Big Bend area of Texas was a unique place prior to the establishment of the National Park not only because of its scenery, but also because of its isolation. The region is blocked on three sides by the Rio Grande, and the rough dirt and caliche roads that ran through the Big Bend were little used because folks did not travel through the area on their way elsewhere. Without modern roads, electricity, and telephones, residents in the Big Bend had to be virtually self-dependent. Loneliness made people friendlier and although neighbors were miles apart, they depended on each other for assistance and companionship.

Surviving in that desolate region was difficult enough, but the Great Depression and a severe drought also plagued the area. For adults it was a time of constant financial worry, frustration, and emotional depression.

Like most residents, Homer Wilson loved the land and desperately struggled to keep it during those economically difficult times when there was little grass and browse for the livestock. He constantly worked to fence and add improvements to his ranch, which included the most beautiful part of the Chisos Mountains. The majestic scenery, however, did not impress the men at the bank and wool house where he borrowed money to keep the ranch operation going. The financial institutions allowed him a limited monthly draw and, like Wilson, they hoped that things would soon get better.

In these difficult times most children did not realize that things were so hard. To them, everyone was in the same condition, and they had no reason to know any better. Toys were scarce, but ingenuity and strong imaginations created all kinds of playthings from the simplest items. Clothing too was improvised with rural boys wearing shirts made of heavy, gray salt sacks, and girls wearing dresses beautifully sewn from patterned cotton flour sacks. All of this goes to show that people can be happy without lots of conveniences.

Homer Wilson's daughter, Patricia Wilson Clothier, helps us understand why her father loved the land and what that struggle was like. She enables us to see life through the eyes of an impressionable and thoughtful youngster in an era where children had time to meditate rather than having activities planned for them every moment of the day. Patricia has vividly retained the memory of a unique lifestyle and of the innumerable little things that make a person appreciate the land.

Today, most visitors to the Big Bend National Park seem to either love the place or hate it. Folks who have grown up there, like Clothier, learned the intricate, beautiful, and fascinating details of the Chihuahuan Desert and never wished to leave. Those of us whose families have lost land to the National Park Service often feel that we have lost part of ourselves. Our hearts ache when we think of those places, special only to us, that we can no longer take care of and love. There is consolation, however, in seeing that what was once "ours" is now enjoyed by many folks who otherwise would never have had the opportunities we once did.

Several authors have written books about the Big Bend, but Clothier's vivid descriptions of the land, people, houses, plants, animals (and aromas associated with all) help visitors gain a new appreciation of the Big Bend and the ranching families that once called it home.

Jack Skiles
Author of *Judge Roy Bean Country*

INTRODUCTION

Homer Wilson, my father, visited the Big Bend as a geologist in 1928. The rugged landscape drew him to the country's mining possibilities. He sold half of his sheep and goat ranch in northern Val Verde County, Texas, to his brother, Earl Wilson, and gave the other half to his mother. In 1929, after arriving in Big Bend to map that country, he began buying land in the Chisos Mountains. Homer expressed the frontier spirit of his ancestors who came early to Collin County, Texas, and then moved westward. If he had wanted to ranch easily and successfully, he would have kept his sixteen-section ranch north of Comstock.

Born in 1892 to T.A. and Bettie Crain Wilson, Homer grew up on the family ranch north of Del Rio, Texas. He graduated from Del Rio High School then attended Rolla School of Mines in Missouri where he earned a degree in Petroleum and Mining Engineering. After serving in World War I as a first lieutenant in the Army Engineers, he went to Carterville, Missouri, as flotation superintendent at a lead and zinc mine before returning to Texas in 1922 to begin his own ranching operation.

As Homer completed plans in the Chisos Mountains, an explosion at the Humble Oil Company in Beaumont killed his former roommate and closest college friend, Willard Pugh, leaving Willard's wife, Bergine, a widow at the age of twenty-six. During their marriage, Willard joked with his wife about his best friend: "If anything ever happens to me, you should marry Old Tex." When Willard died, Bergine was the enrolling clerk of the Texas Legislature, and Homer was 428 miles west of Austin building his forty-four-section ranch.

On April 26, 1929, Homer wrote to her:

> It was awful for a man of Willard's ability to be taken so suddenly from his family and I sincerely feel for you…I may be able to help you in some way as I know quite a few people with the Humble and have a lawyer here…He no doubt has come in contact with accidents very similar to Willard's.

Homer did help with concern and caring. He and Bergine corresponded and visited for the next year and a half. During this time, her sister died and he lost his father and his sister, Edna. These tragedies created a deepening bond.

In 1929, Homer rented a room in Marathon at the Gage Hotel. His quarters also served as an office for ranching and geological business. He lived there and frequently drove the eighty-six miles to his ranch, often leaving Marathon at 4:30 in the morning to travel three or more hours over rough dirt roads.

On a personal level, life improved. Homer and Bergine married on October 4, 1930, in Lake Charles, Louisiana. He, the quiet and ambitious land man, and she, the tall, outspoken sophisticate, now shared the joys and tribulations of living in Big Bend.

* * * * *

I was raised with my parents, Bergine and Homer Wilson, in the Chisos Mountains and surrounding foothills during the 1930s and 1940s. The Wilson ranch contained known landmarks such as the Window, the South Rim, Laguna, and Blue Creek. The present Ross Maxwell Drive in the Big Bend National Park passes through the former Wilson ranch.

An old Park sign at the top of the ridge above Blue Creek headquarters called attention to the lonely life and difficult times experienced by the people who lived in this remote area of southwest Texas. Most, however, do not remember life that way. Stark and difficult at times, life was actually rewarding and fulfilling for those living in Big Bend before the National Park.

Today, many people who come to the Park ask how anyone could have lived there. Since most signs of human habitation have disappeared, it's no wonder the tourists can't imagine life in Big Bend before the Park.

Vivid memories remain of my experiences with frontier life. How people lived, their activities, and their close relationships with neighbors deserve recognition. The strengths and values of these people are worth saving.

I remember life beneath the Window, a cleft in the cliffs of the Chisos Mountains that looked out over the desert where we lived. Growing up in this awesome place gave me a feeling of wonder, a sense of freedom and independence, and a confident assurance when facing life's challenges. Visitors to the National Park may share the beauty and grandeur of this majestic country, but they have difficulty understanding the indomitable courage and resourcefulness of those who carved a way of life from this isolated wilderness.

THE WILSON RANCH

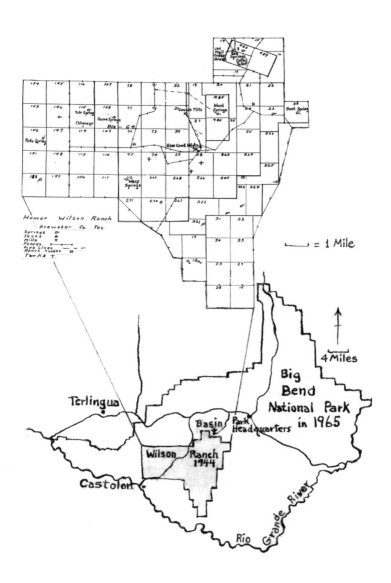

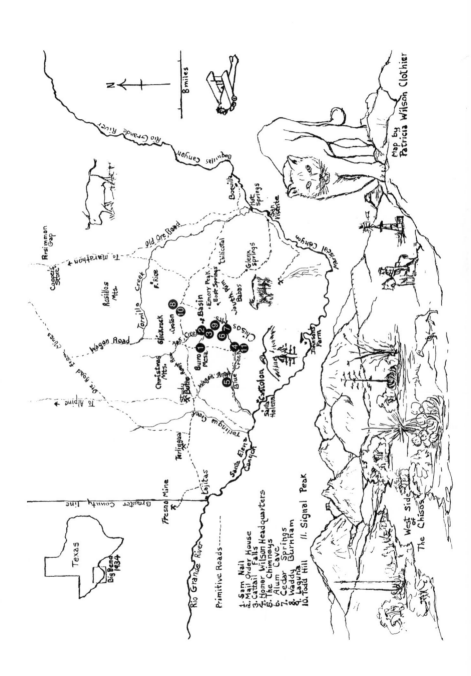

N
8 miles

Rio Grande River

Boquillas Canyon

Boquillas

Hot Springs

Mariscal Canyon

Persimmon Gap

Old Ore Road

To Marathon

Cooper's Store

Rosillos Mts

Tornillo Creek

F. Rice

Emory Peak
Boot Springs
Basin
Chisos
Juniper Canyon
Glenn Springs
Babbs

Mariscal

Ore Road from Alpine

Wagon Road

Slickrock

Christmas Mts

To Alpine

Burro Mesa

Wagon Road
Blue Creek

Santa Elena
Castolon

Terlingua Creek

Terlingua

Santa Elena Canyon

Rio Grande River

Lajitas

Fresno Mine

Brewster County Line

Texas

Big Bend 1934

Primitive Roads ------

1. Sam Nail
2. Mail Order House
3. Cattail Falls
4. Homer Wilson Headquarters
5. The Chimneys
6. Alum Cave
7. Cedar Springs
8. Waddy Burnham
9. Laguna
10. Todd Hill
11. Signal Peak

West Side of The Chisos

Map by Patricia Wilson Clothier

PART I
GOOD TIMES

She draws the light around her
protection from dark shards
of memory, scattered thoughts.
This early light, milky and soft,
reminds her of desert sand
at first dawn. She breathes it in.
Fully awake now, she mounts,
rides her mind into the day's desert,
looks for the next steep climb,
the next place to take herself
to a higher view.

"Invictus Revealed"
Maril Crabtree

Chapter One

A Broader Window

We lurched through the rocky pass at Persimmon Gap that July day in 1936. The purple silhouette of the Chisos Mountains rose some thirty five miles ahead, their craggy edges like paper cutouts in the distance. Cotton clouds with dark undersides floated in the blue sky, casting shadows on the desert floor. Three whirlwinds skipped and leaned as they wound by scrub greasewood, its small, waxed leaves bending and fluttering in the hot wind.

My father drove our pickup truck, his Roi-Tan cigar smoldering as the mid-summer heat blew the sweet, smoky odor across my blonde head and my little brother who lay sleeping on Mother's lap. At five, I sensed an unspoken worry in both my parents: a turned head, grim expression, or a downcast look. I knew they viewed things differently. He saw dreams of minerals and mines while Mother looked at the pink blooms on the sagebrush. She appreciated the stark beauty of the mountains and the elegance of desert plants especially as they bloomed after a rain, covering these hills and valleys with masses of the pink-colored flowers of the sage called ceniza.

As we gained altitude where the road turned west below the mountains, my attention went to the bronze cliffs high above us, guardians of this desert. Daddy motored past Green Gulch, a drainage area into the higher regions. There, pine and drooping juniper trees hugged the pass and grew by rose-colored landslides. I liked the madrone trees in this watershed, their branches showing maroon as the white bark peeled from the trunks and branches. Daddy shifted gears and slowed, the engine hummed to descend the steep incline of Todd Hill. Changing gears again, the pickup jerked over dips and bends then crossed the gravel bed of lower Oak Creek just five miles from home. He looked out over the dry stream bed. "Looks like we got enough rain to bring down the creek, Bergine. I'll have to send Juan down tomorrow to check the fence."

Mother's gaze followed his pointed finger. "We surely needed the rain though. It's a shame we've had so little, and it's been so spotty," she sighed.

Dried limbs caught in the willow roots at the bottom of the arroyo. The bank held leaves and other debris three feet from the gully floor; however, the dry stream showed no other signs of rain. That didn't mean much as streambeds here became dry as soon as the flash flood water disappeared and the sun shone.

Mother seemed lost in thought. "Most of the neighbors are really hurting. Some of their cattle have already died from the drought. I heard the government may start shooting some of the starving cattle if rains don't spread into the lower places."

Daddy grimaced. "We've been lucky here in the mountains where we've had more rain."

I followed her glance from the truck to two javelinas, wild pig-like creatures whose tusked heads grew half as big as their bodies. They turned then ran, their snouts and jaws scarlet from juices of the pitaya cactus growing near the road. I smelled the animal's musky odors and heard them grunt as they topped the hill.

Daddy stopped so I could pick the delicious fruits. I knocked them from the thorn-covered mounds with a stick, rolled each on the ground to remove the prickles, and finally filled my Mexican-straw hat to the brim. As I picked and loaded, I also stood and ate several fresh pitayas, peeling back the red skin that covered the seed-speckled, bright-pink flesh. Their strawberry-like smell floated in the air and juice dripped from my fingers. What a heavenly time, not a moment for imagined troubles.

We turned at our large, pine mailbox that looked like a child's casket. Inside it held mail and a fresh watermelon left for us by friends who farmed on the Rio Grande to the south.

The bumpy, ranch road curved from the county highway over mesquite and lechuguilla-covered hills. Lechuguilla, its foot-high clusters of spine-tipped daggers surrounding a fifteen-foot stalk, accented the rocky area. Daddy told me this plant only grew in the Chihuauan Desert. It liked growing on our place as it covered much of the ground here. Other desert plants mixed with several kinds of cactus and dried grasses. These grasses looked dead, but held nutritious vitamins and minerals.

We slowed for the last descent to the oasis of Oak Creek. Angora goats lounged on the hillside waiting as the Mexican workman put cake (a pressed feed) in the wooden troughs near the stream. The nannies ambled out of the path of our truck, their long, crimped hair hanging close to the ground and swaying as they walked.

Daddy drove past the saddle shed by the terrace of creek stones. This small wooden building also held shoeing supplies and oats for the horses. A lone, bay horse turned his head as we passed, stepping sideways and switching his tail.

Our two-story frame house stood on a terrace formed by a three-foot stone wall and shaded by several tall willow trees. This home rested one mile below the rusty-red cliffs of the Window, a natural opening framing the blue cliffs of Casa Grande and leading to the high mountain areas. The Window overlooked our sanctuary, fifty miles of mesas, desert grasslands, and distant lowlands. This seemed a fairy-tale place to keep us happy and safe.

As my father parked in the shade of the large oaks, the sound of water trickling and flowing through gravel and over rocks joined the rustle of leaves in the late afternoon breeze. The crisp buzz of insects filled the mountain air as my Collie dog, Dusty, barked a welcome.

Daddy strode toward the hired man's adobe house across the creek. Mother carried my brother and I followed as she passed the feathery, salt cedar tree by the screened porch. A prickly-pear cactus edged the wall near the old fig tree. June bugs, their hard shells an iridescent green, tasted the sticky fruits. Nearby, the maguey or century plant grew waiting to send out its one stalk with plates of yellow flower clusters from the blue-gray, agave base. After that, Mother said the plant withers and dies. I thought about that. Why must it go? Other plants bloom and bloom again.

I decided to stay outside with Dusty. After I took off my shoes, I felt the fine gravel on my calloused, bare feet. Then, my dog and I went toward the worktable under the oaks where my father visited in Spanish. Daddy stood a good six inches taller than Juan, who combed his black hair with nervous fingers. My father tipped his sweat-stained, short-brimmed Stetson hat back showing prematurely gray hair, making him look older than his forty-four years. "What happened, Juan?"

"A panther scared the goats at the pens in the night. I heard them bleating, so I ran down there. When I got near, the puma leaped into the arroyo. The Angoras crowded together near that tin shed."

"What about the goats?"

"I was afraid they would pile up and suffocate. None of them died or were killed, though. I stayed down by the pens until dawn in case the panther came back."

"Where did he come from?"

"I'm not sure, Señor."

"What did you do, Juan?"

"Well, I rode up the canyon this morning. Looks like he came through the Window. I didn't see any tracks next to Nail's fence."

"Did you see tracks anywhere else?"

"I found them in the dirt on that second flat place below the old mine. Also, he left paw prints in the sand near the spring."

"Where did he go?"

"He ran from the pens and crawled under the fence by Nail's land, then ran. I fixed that place where the water gap broke last night. He's one big cat, Señor. I'll show you the tracks."

We'll be okay for the night, I think, but he'll be back soon. I'll take those supplies to Blue Creek in the morning and bring some help to work fence starting at the mountain and then around the west side of the section. We'll make it a double one this time so he won't jump it. That won't stop him completely, but might help. I'll set a trap where he went under the fence."

Juan followed to the truck, his pants hanging loose across sandals made of cutout tires with leather thongs. "*Sí, Señor.*"

"Just leave most of those hundred pound sacks of flour, sugar, and frijole beans with the five-gallon cans of lard in the back of the truck, but cover them with that tarp. Put the rice, vermicelli, coffee, and salt in the metal shed. The canned goods go on the back porch for Mrs. Wilson. There's some Bull Durham tobacco for you, hard candy to the muchachos, and thread for your wife in that bag there." Daddy turned and I followed him.

We lived in an old, two-story frame house. Mother told me it was ordered from Sears Roebuck and shipped by train to Marathon, then loaded in marked pieces onto wagons and hauled north of Study Butte for assembly. A man named Rooney took it down and moved it here. In1919 he sold the land to Charlie Burnam, who lived here with his family for about five years until a man named Carter bought the place. Carter tried to raise chickens, but I guess the varmints got them because he finally had to sell to Harris and Winnie Smith. My father bought this area from the Smiths in June of 1929. Sometimes, Mother would get tired of my asking so many questions about our history. Instead, she thought I should know all about country and ranch life.

I didn't have much time to ponder such things as supper was ready on the round oak table by the stairway. This room, the closest thing we had to a living room, had the furniture Mother brought when she and Daddy married, including a green velour chaise lounge with walnut trim, a wing chair someone had made for her, and a big, oak rocker with a dark-red leather seat. Mother loved beautiful things, but didn't have much of a place for them here. Most of what we had was what my daddy called "practical."

After supper, we all sat on the iron beds that lined the porch wall, except my younger brother, who played with his little metal cars outside. His real name is Homer Junior, but we called him Buzzy because he made bee sounds as he pushed his cars in the dirt.

Mother and Daddy paid little attention to me, but I listened as they talked.

"What's the matter, Homer?" Mother's big, brown eyes showed concern.

"A panther came down by the pens last night, Bergine. It's bad enough we lost several hundred sheep to mountain lions this year without them getting our registered goats too. Those cats seem to kill for the fun of it. The last six kills weren't eaten at all. The panther didn't even drag any brush to cover the dead bodies like they do when they're coming back for a meal."

"What are you going to do?" Her voice soothed and sympathized.

"When I take the supplies to Blue Creek tomorrow, I'll get several of the men and we'll work fence and set traps. It seems like I fix one thing and something else goes wrong. It's a constant battle with nature. We are so isolated and the country's a regular Outback here."

"I know, Homer, but you're improving the place all the time. Think about that. You've fenced, piped water, built tanks, and made roads. I know the varmints are terrible, but you'll figure that out too."

Daddy often talked about our varmint troubles. Predators plagued other livestock. Cattle and horse raisers lost calves and colts to mountain lions. These panthers played with their prey. A big cat, often six to nine feet long, crept up to a herd of sheep, leaped on an unsuspecting animal, and broke the animal's back with one bite. Since the ranch bordered Mexico, these cats crossed the river and the battle never ended.

Coyotes killed our livestock too. They, however, ate their kills and could be controlled with fencing and trapping. Bobcats and bear gave us fewer problems. Another predator, the eagle, with a wingspread of over six feet, would land on a high point, and then search the surrounding area for live food. An eagle trap was placed on a wooden cross above the house at Oak Creek. If an eagle landed, the trap caught, held it, and the baby goats survived another night.

Daddy told me he lost over 1,500 sheep and goats from his 8,000 animals the year before. This terrible loss caused him to declare war on predators. "My sheep and goats have a right to live too!"

My thoughts drifted back to Mother and Daddy's conversation.

"I know, but you love it here, Homer, and so do I. It will work. I know it will. You always fix things. How you manage is beyond me, but you do. You've taken an untamed country and made a good ranch out of it. Not many can do what you've done."

"It's time, Bergine. It's time that's lacking. I have so much to do. Things don't stay fixed. There's no one to put part of the responsibility on. The ranch is our bread and butter, but working those mining claims is important too. I didn't spend four years studying mining engineering for nothing."

"This is our home now. I know you think ranching is your way to earn a living and geology is your life's work, but you can do both. At least, that's what you said. We're all working for a better life for our families, whatever problems nature sends us."

"You're right, Bergine. I just get so frustrated sometimes."

I looked through the screen as their voices faded in my mind. The Chisos Mountains glowed as the setting sun flamed yellow, orange, and then deep maroon and purple. The eastern moon showed through the opening in the mountains as it looked down and across the magnificent desert and at life beneath the Window. When day turned to night and Mother lit the kerosene lamps, stars twinkled like a million fireflies in a sky of dark-blue velvet. The mountain canyons echoed the distant, wild scream of the mountain lion.

Chapter Two

ROUGH COUNTRY

A misty blue blurred the sharpness of the Window and its surrounding bluffs. I heard the slam of the oven door and smelled the aroma of hot biscuits and slab bacon as I pulled on my jeans and laced my brogans. My father insisted these were the safest shoes for protection from sharp rocks and thorns. We certainly had plenty of those here. Actually, the brown, tough leather didn't look bad though it was scratched and scraped. Clothes didn't mean much to me, but I liked wearing shoes like my dad's.

After breakfast, Daddy and I walked to the pens to meet the workman. The panther's paw prints showed the big cat had paced back and forth by the south edge of the gate to the enclosure. At one place you could see where the cougar heard the hired man and lept towards the creek and Nail's fence. We picked our way through rocks and boulders. Here and there we saw more marks in the sand. At this point, the stream water sank into the gravel, leaving no signs of the fresh, cold liquid flowing beneath the surface.

We approached the woven wire across the arroyo where

my father crouched. Here he pulled on his worn leather gloves over the edge of his long-sleeved, khaki shirt. He also wore dun-colored pants to disguise any dirt.

"This looks like a good place for that trap. Get one of those larger sotol poles, will you, Juan?"

Daddy dug a hole for the set trap, placed it with care, and covered it with fine dirt sieved through a piece of window screen. Then, brushing the area with a leafed branch, he leaned the wooden pole about two and a half feet over the swept spot.

"What's that stalk for, Daddy?"

"That's to warn people like you that I've set a trap under the pole." His eyes crinkled, and he smiled.

I did wonder about the people who might not know his signals. However, they weren't supposed to wander around down here and probably wouldn't since it was twelve miles to Burnham's and the Nails knew about Daddy's traps.

"That's all we can do right now. Don't touch anything here, Patricia, or the panther will smell you and shy away from here."

I didn't need that warning as the whole area scared me.

My father and the workman strode to the pickup truck as I ran ahead to play. The mourning doves cooed when I waved to Maria, the hired man's wife. She sat in the adobe house doorway with her two small children. The smoke from her campfire spiraled in the morning air, wafting the odor of burning mesquite across the creek.

I passed our house, then skipped along the path from the back porch to the old, unused outhouse near the dump area east of the metal utility building and entered the dim, wooden structure to play. A daddy longlegs, with his legs pulsating, climbed the shadowed corner. As I turned around on the seat and looked down toward the floor, an enormous diamondback rattlesnake was coiled in the corner ready to strike — his dark-patterned body seemed as fat as my arm. I froze. My body shrank against the wooden wall behind the shelf's two cutout holes. The angry whir filled the dark room. His tongue flicked in and out as if tasting the air. His hooded eyes glinted in the reflected light as I leaped to the platform corner.

"Help! Daddy, help!" I screamed. Mother wouldn't know what to do if I called her. "It's a rattlesnake. Help!"

Usually, I rescued myself, but if I jumped through the open door, the rattler might strike me. I was trapped. If only Daddy heard me.

"I'm coming! Don't move!" He answered my yells.

Daddy's footsteps crunched down the rocky path. He paused outside the open plank door, took aim with his pistol, and shot the rattler in the head. Its body writhed on the floor making scratching sounds on the dusty wood. When my father snatched me from the dangerous shelf, I threw my legs around his waist and clung to his shoulders, my heart thumping against his chest. He smelled of familiar soap and tobacco. I felt lucky and safe after he rescued me since he often worked other places on the ranch this part of the year.

Most of the time, snakes stayed away from our yard. We kept a dog to bark a warning and cats to kill mice that drew snakes, but that didn't solve all our reptile problems. Mother remembered an incident from the past:

> One evening we came home and there really was a rattlesnake coiled up in that big rocker in the dining room. I guess it got in through the back porch. That porch wasn't too good. It probably crawled under the door or something like that. Well, I don't remember whether Homer shot it or what he did. When I came back, it was gone.

I guess Mother cringed and ran out of the room. She never could stand snakes.

Frederick Rice told about his experiences with snakes when he was a boy at Grapevine, a few miles north of the Chisos Mountains. Stanley Ewald wrote about Mr. Rice's experiences in his book, *My Name Is Frederick Rice and I Was Born Here.*

There were a good many rattlesnakes around when I was a boy. We had rattlesnakes all right! We had a horse bit just this side of Grapevine one morning…Daddy loped off to the Grapevine house and he got a quart of coal oil and a piece of an old blue shirt, and he rode back.

He took some daggers…the yucca. Well, he cut some daggers and he jabbed it in, and throwed them down and cut more and jabbed them in…so he'd bleed, see? So the poison would come out. He done this several times, and then he tied this old blue shirt around it, and he poured that coal oil on it. I remember he bandaged it all the way to the shoulder. And the horse got All Right!!

We would sleep on the ground, and weren't afraid of 'em. They say if you get a hair rope, and stretch that rope on the ground, well, the snakes won't cross it. But I don't believe that…I don't remember of any white people…or Mexicans either…getting bit by a rattlesnake.

* * * * *

Since Daddy planned a quick trip to headquarters at Blue Creek, Mother, Buzzy, and I went too. Dusty and I rode in the back of the pickup as we jolted the two miles to our closest neighbors, the Nail family.

The Nails' adobe home was nestled in some willow trees at the foot of Burro Mesa. Daddy stayed outside to talk about that panther-proof fence with Sam, who strode toward us. This tall, thin, friendly neighbor's eyes sparkled. His hat sat sideways on his head. Mother said that made him look rakish. Most of what Mr. Nail said was right, but he did like to tell stories, especially to young people like me.

I usually checked his tales with Julia, his daughter.
Mother's cotton dress blew in the sunny breeze. Nena
Nail, her peppered-gray hair in a little bun, met us with a
shy, warm smile. Mrs. Nail's natural quietness balanced Mr.
Nail's outgoing personality. She was a good listener to
Mother, who also liked to tell stories. As they went indoors
to visit, I ran to Julia.

I called Julia my sister, and I loved her dearly. Though
timid and quiet with others, she showered me with love.
That is, even though she was fifteen, she spent time with me,
played with me, let me hug her, and listened as I told her
about the snake in the outhouse and the panther tracks at the
pens. We crossed the shaded patio of flagstones at the back of
the house, her arm draped across my shoulders. I went to the
hand-dug well that was about ten feet deep, ten feet across,
and lined with rock. As we leaned over and watched the
frogs, a small snake rested on a stone shelf near the bottom of
the well. Dragonflies buzzed and the sound of a pebble plop-
ping in the water echoed in the reservoir. Snapdragons
bloomed in Mrs. Nail's flowerbeds beside this sheltered spot,
giving a faint, sweet fragrance. Earlier, lavender and purple
violets filled the shady spots near the flagstones. Birds sang
to one another from the willow branches as the narrow limbs
swayed and the green leaves rustled.

Mother called, and the magic faded. "We have to go now,
but Nena asked us to supper. So, you'll see Julia again this
evening."

We bumped and bounced toward Blue Creek, passing the
beehives near the white brush in the draw on our right. The
lingering odor of these flowers drifted by the truck. Bees
made the best honey from white brush nectar. Many sounds
reached me. The windmills clanked and a burro brayed as
we passed the enclosures at the shearing pens below Ward
Mountain. A few sheep drank from the trough by the water
tank. Others lounged under the mesquite trees in the dap-
pled shade. Just two more miles up rocky hills and we
descended to the cement house at headquarters, marked in

the background by Signal Peak, its three graduated rims tiered to a point where I imagined Indians of long ago sent smoke signals seen past the Rio Grande River to our south. We parked near the hitching post where our new foreman, Lott Felts, met us. Mr. Felts, all business, nodded and spoke to Mother, but didn't seem to notice me. I saw Mrs. Felts at the door to the house, a white sugar sack tied around her plump waist. She looked like she was listening with her head turned slightly to one side. In her hands she carried a large pan of homemade cornbread for their four hunting hounds. She set the bread outside on the wooden bench beneath the young cottonwood tree.

Mother said we needed to build a bigger house here at headquarters as soon as we had a little money as this one seemed too small for Mr. and Mrs. Felts, their son, and daughters, Lunetta and Frances. Lunetta, the Felts' blonde teenager, worked for us as a hired hand when we needed her. Frances, a dark-haired, confident girl, looked several years older and larger than myself. She dominated our play. Being small and thin for my age had its drawbacks.

After lunch of frijole beans, goat meat, and sliced tomato with onions and cucumbers, Frances and I went down to see a coyote pelt in the sand of Blue Creek. The trapper had stretched the skin over an A-shaped, wooden frame, leaving the salted, sand-filled fur to dry in the hot summer sun. I talked to Frances about the mountain lion problem at Oak Creek, and she seemed properly impressed.

Before we left for home, Daddy told Mr. Felts he needed several men to build the panther-proof fence at Oak Creek.

"What's a panther-proof fence, Daddy?"

"We add a two- to three-foot layer of woven wire to the top of the fence we already have. This new, top part leans outward toward Nail's pasture. It keeps predators away from our land."

I knew panthers killed our sheep and goats, but wasn't sure this fence could solve our problems, especially if they climbed through the pass at the Window where a bluff was a barrier. I knew cougars could get by that bluff.

Mr. Felts suggested sending Art Hannold and a Mexican man in the International truck with rolls of wire the next day, though this left Mr. Felts short-handed for a few days. Art was my favorite workman. He teased, but he always noticed me and I liked that. His eyes crinkled at the corners when he laughed, and his black hair fell across his forehead. Leather chaps hung low at his waist and showed a large, silver buckle on his belt.

Art brought me orphan creatures that he found while riding in the pastures. As a result, I had a baby rabbit, a little rock squirrel, and a pet deer at different times. My pet deer followed me everywhere. When he grew horns, he reared on his hind legs and brought his sharp, pointed hooves down toward my head. He was just playing, but my father thought the young buck dangerous. He and Art took my treasured pet to the other side of the ranch where they turned him loose to lead a wild life.

The story about Art's life before he came to our place fascinated me. In 1933 he rode into Mexico after some of his horses had strayed across the Rio Grande. Border authorities gave Art permission to hunt for his animals in Mexico where he and a friend rode into a trap. Mexican lawmen captured and falsely imprisoned them about twenty miles from the Rio Grande. Art's father telegraphed for government help. Finally, the mayor at Ocampo sent a message and returned the two to Boquillas. This mayor said the real culprits, Candelario Baiza and his bandits, drove the horses across the Rio Grande and evaded capture. My father called this abduction an international incident.

Mother told me a story about Art's younger sister, Lucy, and brother, Bill. Lucy and Bill stayed alone on their place by Tornillo Creek at the time of Pancho Villa and his outlaw raids in about 1912. Art and his father had business elsewhere for several months. During this time the children, who were about seven and nine, hunted rabbits for food. Once they hid on the roof when they heard a rider approach, fearing bandits. Thrilling things happened all the time in Big Bend, but Mother said she can do with a little less sensation.

Others in Big Bend kept wild pets. Elinor Cartledge whose father, Robert, ran the Chisos Mine at Terlingua, remembered her deer. Sometime after she started going out for the school year, her father took some folks on a hunting trip into Chihuahua, Mexico, across from Castolon. Someone in the party killed a doe by mistake leaving an orphaned baby deer. Her father brought the animal home to the mine at Terlingua. Elinor told me the story.

> We had a large fenced backyard so that was where we raised the deer. When the deer got big enough to carry our weight, my sister and I loved to mount the deer and ride it. Obviously the deer did not really like it all that well. When the deer grew to a large buck, he was taken to Uncle Wayne's at Castolon. For several years the buck stayed around the complex there and whenever we drove in to spend the day with cousin Gene, Aunt Josephine and Uncle Wayne, the buck recognized our car and, as soon as Nancy and I got out of the car, we had to head quickly for their fenced yard or else we were in for a butting. Talk about good memory. After quite a few years of staying there at Castolon to be fed with other stock, the buck got nature's call to the wild for mature activity and ran for the hills never more to be seen. I always hoped no hunter ever brought the deer down despite his animosity toward Nancy and me.

Daddy honked the pickup's horn, calling me from remembered stories of wild pets. Buzzy and I scrambled into the truck bed for the trip back to Nail's. Present times and future dreams rode with us in the shadows of the Chisos foothills.

Chapter Three

ILLUSIVE DREAMS

When we arrived at Nail's, I helped Julia set the table in the visiting room. The whitewashed adobe walls and pine-beamed ceiling covered with sotol poles kept the room cool in July. Julia liked things festive, so we decorated the dinner plates with violet leaves from the patio garden. We laughed and talked together, her dark hair pulled back from her face, and the glow from the carbide lights glinted on her eyes. Julia, a kind and patient person, helped me do the silverware properly. Smells of homemade rolls baking in the wood stove and peach cobbler cooling filled the room as we placed the hand-edged, cloth napkins. Mother and Mrs. Nail talked as they fixed supper in the kitchen.

"Do you remember, Nena, how people around Marathon bet we wouldn't last six months out here in this rough country when we first came?"

"I'm sure they don't think that now, Bergine."

"I certainly didn't know much about country life, let alone west Texas living. All those mistakes! When someone grows up here they automatically know what to say and do.

It seemed like I did everything wrong. Problems began when I insulted your relative, Mr. Todd. As I went for a stroll in Marathon, he sat on the edge of that boardwalk. I saw an old man with a long, gray beard. He asked if it rained out in our country. I huffed back to the hotel to tell Homer about this forward man. When I told Homer, he looked dismayed and said, 'What did he look like?' "

"Oh, dear, Bergine," Nena sighed.

"When I described Mr. Todd, Homer clenched his teeth and whispered. 'Oh, no. That's our neighbor,' as he ran to apologize and explain. How was I to know that asking about the weather was a friendly and important conversation out here?"

"He didn't mind, Bergine. He knew you didn't grow up here." Nena smiled as she lifted the pan of hot rolls from the oven."

Mother stirred the pot of green beans with a wooden spoon. "Well, the way I think about it is the one who comes from the city into the Big Bend doesn't know anything about all this out here and tries her very best to show her husband that she can stick it out. The girl from the city bends over backwards to succeed, and she's so dumb that she doesn't know all these things a girl raised on a ranch knows immediately. When we came here, we didn't know that people in Marathon thought we would fail."

"Don't say that. We know you belong here. You add excitement and a new way of seeing to our lives."

"I don't know about that. Well, anyway, another time Homer introduced me to a gentleman. I said, 'Oh, I'm so glad to meet you. I hear you're such a good veterinarian.' The poor doctor looked bewildered. Homer told me previously, 'He's just a horse doctor is all he is.'"

"Ha. Ha! I can imagine what Homer thought when you did that."

"Nena, I don't know why anyone puts up with me. I seem to do so many wrong things."

"They like you, Bergine. You're friendly and helpful.

People around here don't mind if you grew up in the city or out here. They know you care about them, and that's all that matters."

"You've been a good friend and such a comfort. I don't know what I would do without you. You're always there when we need you. Remember when Patricia was three and got lost at Oak Canyon? I sent a frantic message for help and all of you came. We walked up and down the creek calling her name, but she didn't say anything. It was Julia who coaxed Patricia to answer. She sat by the little irrigation ditch beyond the peach trees where the brush hid her from the creek."

Nena smiled. "As I remember, she splashed and played in the water. Patricia looked like she knew exactly where she was and what she was doing, but it is dangerous when a child's lost with so many rocks and snakes."

Mother laughed at that. She often accused me of being independent. Sometimes she called me a "tomboy," making that sound like something with rough edges.

"Nena, remember when Buzzy swallowed a rough, pointed peach seed, and you rushed to Oak Creek again? Former President Wilson's grandson, Dean Sayer, visited at your house at the time and drove you that day. Mr. Sayer said, 'Feed him some bread.' You suggested oatmeal to coat the peach stone. For safety, I fed him both. The crisis passed and he survived."

"We help each other, Bergine." Nena covered the hot rolls with a linen napkin.

Julia and I carried the heaping bowls of fresh green beans, mashed potatoes, steaming gravy, frijoles, and bread with hand-churned butter. We all sat at the table, though Buzzy needed a little box to reach his plate.

After supper and goodbyes, we started home to Oak Creek. The setting sun turned the approaching mountains bright orange. The hills, shaded at sunset, seemed a dark maroon, with golden highlights on an occasional sotol stalk.

* * * * *

Mother said she didn't mind the rough country living, but she did worry about medical help in times of crisis. The closest hospital was 200 miles from the ranch. It wasn't bad if you had a case of poison ivy or got impetigo in a scrape or cut, but anything more serious caused anxiety. When I was three my dog bit me. Sport foamed at the mouth and staggered until he fell near the porch. After he died, my father sent my pet's head to Austin. Lab results showed rabies. This forced our family to go there, the closest place for the required shots, more than 400 miles from home. The doctors gave me injections in my stomach each day for three weeks. Rabies proved a killer if you didn't do this. Daddy said we were lucky they had the shots now. At the age of ten, a wild fox bit him. His parents used a mad stone, the gallstone of a deer, to draw out the poison. I guess they didn't have rabies shots then. Anyway, he lived.

Another medical crisis happened when Mother was expecting my baby brother. Mother told me what happened back then.

> I got so that if I walked from the kitchen at Oak Creek to put something on the dining room table, I had to grasp the walls and furniture to get to the table. When these waves of blackness came, I thought I was dying. Area doctors said I had malnutrition. So, I went home to my family in St. Louis and took you with me. When I got there, I was so swollen I broke the silk hose on my legs. I went straight to the hospital and had the baby. I had a raging temperature, but the doctors had trouble figuring what was wrong. Finally, an intern at Barnes Hospital said, "You look like you have malaria." I did have malaria and so did you, Patricia. Your orange coloring wasn't from eating carrots out of the garden like that other doctor

said. Finally, we got the new medicines, Atabrine and Plasmoquin, from Dr. Brinkley in Del Rio. They were miracle drugs for us.

* * * * *

The Victorino family of parents and eleven of their twelve children lived at Blue Creek in 1932. The oldest son, Simón, worked at Oak Creek at that time. Some of the younger Victorinos also did ranch work. Mother told me about an incident with Simón:

I just thought that Homer was dead some place or along the road hurt when he didn't come home one night. I went over across the creek where Simón Victorino lived and I knocked and knocked on the doorway of the adobe. He didn't answer, so I decided I'd just have to go in and wake him. Well, when I started through the door and I saw him, it was such a sight. He was so big in his white underwear. They wore white, heavy-cotton, long shirts and long pants. He got up and he took me to headquarters. It was beginning to be daylight when we got there. In that old car, it took over an hour to get over to that gravel at the bottom of the Blue Creek hill where the car stuck in the sand and gravel. I said in English that I'd walk, and Simón could tell by the way I talked what I meant. He didn't understand English and I didn't understand Spanish, but he got out and just picked that car up and turned it around. He was so big and strong and healthy.

When Homer came, he was furious with me. It didn't help when I told him I thought he was dead. He was always going off doing geology and staying for six days when he told me he'd be back in two. He'd say, "I'm not going to let you know when I'm coming back, and expect me when you see me coming."

One day, Chano Victorino, one of our best laborers and a younger brother to Simón, worked at the head of Blue Creek in the mountainous area we called "On Top" where he and another brother worked goats under herd. Tall grass waved near gnarled oaks and the cliffs of the canyon looked cobalt blue in the distance.

The younger Victorino boy fell into the water tank. Although neither of the men swam, Chano jumped in the reservoir to save his younger brother. He grabbed him and shoved him to safety. Instead of reaching for Chano, the younger brother panicked and ran for help. He fled the more than five miles down the mountains to the Blue Creek headquarters. When other Victorinos scrambled and raced to the tank, they found Chano drowned. They carried his limp and lifeless body by mule over the trail of switchbacks to the tents at headquarters.

The oldest brother, Simón, took Chano by pickup truck along the old wagon road down Blue Creek by way of Wasp Spring the twenty-seven miles to Terlingua. Mr. Nail transported the rest of the Victorino family, as my father had left to do geology before the accident. They buried Chano in the cemetery outside this small mining town, covering the beige mound with stones and placing a wooden cross at the head of the grave.

As Simón returned to the ranch, the truck stalled in an arroyo bed. He decided to check the gasoline level. After he lit a match and looked in the gas tank, the fumes exploded and burned him below the waist.

When Daddy told Mother that Simón suffered serious burns from the explosion, Mother agonized. "We've got to get him to a doctor, Homer."

"They won't let us get a doctor, Bergine."

"We just have to. We can't leave him like that."

So, Mother went over to headquarters with Daddy. Simón

sat in front of the tent with his burned legs stretched out in the sun. The Victorino parents refused to let my mother and father take Simón for medical help. Each day they carried him and seated him in the sunshine, and he recovered after several months of this ultraviolet treatment.

After Simón regained his health, he heard about a better-paying job in the quicksilver mines at Terlingua where they mined cinnabar and later processed it into mercury. Simón worked in those deep, dusty passageways and caverns for about two years. Some of the tunnels reached 600-foot depths. This tall, strong man, who once lifted a Model T stuck in gravel and sand, died of lung disease. No home remedy or healer cured something like this.

Despite pain from accidents and disease, and losses from hard times and rough nature, ranchers, workers, friends, and neighbors of Big Bend lived and died with grace. These were strong, caring, and resourceful people. Their inner strength, like the mesquite tree, had roots reaching within the earth as much as five times deeper than the tree was tall.

Chapter Four

BENEATH THE WINDOW

Alone rider edged his way across the landslide by the Window as the morning sun poured through the over-look like white gold. The clink of horseshoes against stone signaled that only one mile remained to our house. Ira Hector, the only person I knew who dared ride a horse from the Basin across slabs of treacherous rocks, inched his way over the trail past the old mine. Ira ran cattle and horses on his land that joined ours at the Basin, the bowl-like valley nestled in the mountains. Once a month he rode the ninety-six miles to Alpine to see his wife and family. He always came to our house first and ate with us before he went on to the Nails' place. Sometimes he arrived at their house in the middle of the night, and they fed him whenever he arrived. Then, he'd stop at Study Butte and Terlingua. From there, he visited people along the way to Alpine.

When he passed the point where Daddy, Art Hannold, and another workman fixed the added layer of fence, Mr. Hector stopped. By this time the sun hung high, so the men quit for lunch then rode to our house. Ira seemed old, but he was middle aged, the cowboy type, tall, angular, and thin. His brown face and hands looked like worn saddle leather. As the men visited on the front porch, I helped Mother in the kitchen. She added extra mesquite to the cast-iron stove, stepping around the wood-chip box beside the enamel sink. Frijole beans simmered, leftover goat meat warmed with garden carrots in the oven, and a large pot of water waited to boil the fresh corn on the cob from our garden. I carried the bottle of chili petines (tiny varicolored peppers with vinegar) and a saucer of sliced onions to the oilcloth-covered table in the dining room then returned past the large rocking chair. Mother said she felt average sized in this rocker. My father's six feet matched her five feet ten and one half inch height.

When I returned to the kitchen, she let me cut out the biscuits with an aluminum cookie cutter, then fill the flat pan with dough rounds before she placed it in the oven. I hurried to the cooler on the back porch for milk and butter. For dessert she served Ruby's Pie, a rough-textured cheesecake made with cottage cheese and cinnamon. The bowl of freshly-sliced, sugar-coated peaches also seemed a dessert. The breeze from the propped-open doors cooled us as we ate, although at a 4,400-foot altitude we enjoyed temperatures twenty degrees less than the desert lowlands.

Ira thanked Mother for the meal, his hands twisting and turning his hat. Then he mounted his bay horse and left for Nail's, while Daddy and the other men returned to their woven-wire project.

Mother told me, "I wonder how Nena feels with more unexpected company. Contrary to what people think, we have many visitors here, and we never know how long they'll stay. I told her once that a man came to see them for a day and stayed for three years."

I guess Mother was right since Julia gave me a similar idea. "When your father let someone go, he just came over to our place and stayed. The one who stayed three years was about seven feet tall and extremely homely. I don't think he was too bright either, but he had a very good heart. Daddy hated to send anyone away in need."

One middle-aged man kept arriving at Oak Creek at mealtime. Mother decided to do something about this problem. She found he didn't like onions. So, whenever he visited, Mother cooked with onions. At first he said, "No thank you." Then as he became very hungry, he'd have to eat them. So, she told Mrs. Nail, "Now you fix onions too, and he'll have a different route," because he came to our place and then went to her house. I don't think Nena did this though. Some people might think we didn't have any excitement down in our country, but we had plenty in the Chisos.

Mother enjoyed the interesting people who visited, but worried about so many strangers arriving. Many came to explore or do research, at times digging for artifacts in caves on our ranch. Others stayed with us, bringing back their finds as well as silt from these shelters. She asked Dr. Johnson of Del Rio about the dangers of exposure to germs. He told her, "Watch out, Bergine! It can be a hundred years later and the tuberculosis germ from those cave inhabitants will still be alive. It has a wax-like coating, and takes at least twenty minutes of heat to kill it. The thing to do is take the mattresses out in the open and let them stay in the hot sun. This kills the germs." This did little to decrease her anxiety, but certainly increased her workload.

I liked these talks while we worked even though I didn't like doing the dishes. We had running water piped from a wooden barrel at the end of the irrigation ditch that wound around the hill east of the house past the two peach orchards and the vegetable garden. The clear water flowed above the creek to the springs one-half mile up Oak Canyon. Icy-cold, this had a high concentration of fluoride that caused white spots on my teeth and brown streaks on the teeth enamel of others. Daddy told me this mineral thickened our teeth enamel though. He and Mother tried hauling other drinking water without the mineral, but stopped this when they found me drinking out of the creek.

* * * * *

When Evelyn Burnam, Julia's older cousin who once lived at Oak Creek, visited headquarters, she recalled living in the Chisos.

When I was born in 1918, my mother, father, and sister lived in the mail-order house you live in now. This was a beautiful area, and the little stream continued on through oak trees growing wild in front of the house. The front porch was screened and covered with vines. Blackberries grew on the west side of the house — also flowers and many butterflies, which I was always trying to catch. At times we encountered snakes — some copperhead, but mostly rattlesnakes. All of our lives, when we children started anywhere, there was an admonition to watch out for snakes.

Bob and Julia Nail were our main playmates. We went to their house often or they came to ours. We had other cousins living at the Burnham's house at what is called Government Springs, but we didn't see them often. The roads were all dirt and we didn't use the car unnecessarily as we got a spare five-gallon can of gas when we were in town and we usually needed it to get back to town.

We had no refrigeration or electricity, so we had very little meat except in cold weather. People butchered a cow, a hog, or a goat, and shared with their neighbors, and the neighbors did likewise when they butchered. A portion of the beef was always cut in strips, salted and peppered, and hung in a little smoke house to be smoked and dried. We kept a few chickens and my father milked a cow. I vaguely remember that we had a man and his wife working most of the time. The woman helped in the house, and the man helped my father with the cattle and garden and general work. I think we only had this help when we were very small as my mother was sick quite a lot. Later, my father just hired someone to help him when he couldn't do everything by himself. He spent all of his money in order that my mother could go back to her folks in Minnesota for an operation. My mother never really adjusted to the isolated Texas life and developed a mental problem after she returned from the surgery. She returned to Minnesota another time, and my father had to sell everything to pay expenses.

Things had not changed much since Evelyn lived here. Daddy built a septic tank for the bathroom so we didn't use the old outhouse. A chicken house kept the fowl safe at night, and we added a storage building for supplies. The adobe worker's house still stood across the creek. We no longer had a smoke house, so we didn't smoke-dry meat. In fact, Mother and Mrs. Nail didn't can meat or bland vegetables. They worried the high altitude wouldn't process these properly as water boils at a lower temperature here, and we might get ptomaine poisoning. Daddy did erect a wind charger — a windmill device to generate electricity — at the top of the hill west of the house. This gave enough power to run our Zenith radio.

Unfortunately, the static from the mountains interfered with reception from the radio stations at Del Rio and in Mexico, the only two stations we could hear in Big Bend. One time, Mother did get fair reception while Daddy was home. Daddy heard Dr. Brinkley, the goat-gland doctor who aired a daily radio program promoting his goat-gland transplant to rejuvenate aging males, say on his morning program, "Are you a joy to your wife?" Daddy, a bit of a puritan about such matters, held conservative opinions about many things. When they first married, he objected to Mother wearing her lovely, black lace underwear though others did not see it. This time he glowered at her. "I don't know if I should be angry with Brinkley for his lousy sales pitch or at you for listening to such a program!" Daddy didn't yell, he just seemed furious.

Mother didn't have much time for the radio. Household tasks took more time then than they do today. She washed clothes much the same as others did. Mother carried the baskets to the area past the woodpile where she boiled several cans and pots of water. Some people cleaned their clothes every Monday, but not Mother. We washed when we had several loads of dirty things. She scrubbed the pieces on a washboard and ran them through a ringer into tubs of clean water for rinsing. Daddy taught her how to clean his khaki pants on a wooden bench with a scrub brush. I can still see her bent over the bench, brush in hand, white suds soaking into the beige pants legs. She boiled the white sheets in an iron container over the fire. I took care of Buzzy as his curious nature often drew him to the bubbling pot. The fresh smell of clean clothes flapping free on the lines filled the morning air before she gathered them into a basket and carried them to the house.

* * * * *

Before shearing in August, Daddy left for roundup at Blue Creek. Our daily life settled into a routine without my father, much of which included ranch activities. Sometimes I watched the Mexican man milk the Jersey cow. White streams of steaming, rich milk pinged against the sides of the large pail. Mother cooled our can and skimmed the thick cream. Then she made cottage cheese from clabbered milk, soured in a pan with a little vinegar then hung in a clean sugar sack on the clothesline outside. The whey dripped until nothing but cottage cheese stayed in the bag.

The Mexican worker shod the horses at the saddle shed

near the wooden gate. He held the animal's leg between his knees and filed the foot's horny covering smooth. When he attached the metal horseshoe, the bright sun glinted off the new nails as he pounded them on an angle through the holes and into the hoof. I smelled oats for the horses, saddle leather from the stored tack, and the pungent odor of wet tobacco. The gunny sacking felt rough beneath my tanned hands. Suddenly, a scorpion stung my bare foot. I jumped and grabbed my ankle. The workman quickly made a poultice of his tobacco. This home remedy worked as I had little pain and no complications. Many people in Big Bend used home remedies.

Late that afternoon, the hired man let me ride in the old spring wagon. He hitched two mules to the wood and metal tongue, and we jostled and tipped through gullies to Cattail Canyon. There he dug mesquite roots and loaded dead wood that washed down from the mountains. Smells of damp leaves and dirt floated near the wagon as my jeans pocket bulged with found treasures of sparkling rocks, bleached bones, and gray feathers. When the wagon bed was filled with limbs, we bumped back to Oak Creek where he dumped the load at the woodpile.

Other ranch work needed doing at Oak Creek. The buck sheep, also called rams, lived in the trap northeast of the house. Since the bucks fought continually, the hired hand had to roundup these registered sheep every three days then treat their wounds with tecole, a foul-smelling disinfectant used to fight screwworms. When two bucks backed off from each other, lowered their coiled horns, than ran head-on, crashing their foreheads together, the cracking noise of their skulls thundered through the canyons. The resulting head wounds drew flies that laid eggs on the scrapes and sores. If the wounds went untreated, the eggs hatched and screw-shaped worms ate the exposed flesh, killing these valuable animals. Since the sores re-infected as the medicine wore away, these sheep needed constant attention. The bucks were only out of this pasture when sheared or when put with the ewes in the fall for mating.

Registered billy goats also stayed in this pasture at Oak Creek. Their long, curly hair hung to the ground. They turned to look at me, their proud heads with curled horns held high. The nanny goats flourished in the larger pasture that included Cattail Falls. At night they drifted back to the hill by the road. Here they rested and waited, wavy white hair like pillows on the rocks. As the sun splayed golden light on the tops of hills and trees, they strolled down to the pens to their kids.

The last fenced enclosure held little A-frame shelters for the young goats called sanchos. Each kid's hoof, attached by rope to a metal ring, allowed it some freedom. The shelter shaded these youngsters during the hot times, letting the nannies forage and browse. If the kids went with the mothers, eagles would kill more of the little goats. I remember watching as each mother found her own offspring by sound, sight, and smell, then let him nurse. The young kid would kneel on his front hooves with his little back legs straight, all the while wagging his tuft of tail, happy that Mother came. Those afternoons always seemed to have a gentle breeze that ruffled the curly white mohair of the kid and its mother, and as the shadows would lengthen across the pens, the late afternoon sun would brush the tops of the hills with a peaceful, copper glow.

After the evening chores, Buzzy played in the creek near the Mexican house. My brother built roads for his cars in the earthen bank. I walked toward the terrace edged in stones where the adobe-brick house stood. It had a corner fireplace in the one room used for sleeping as well as living. This hearth gave warmth to cold nights. In hot weather, most cooking was done outdoors over a campfire. Maria mixed bread dough in an enamel pan of flour, baking powder and a salt mixture on the wooden table under the west window. The wooden window shutters opened into the room, and the open door let in a brisk breeze. She poured hot grease into a depression in the flour, and then stirred the mixture until all oil absorbed the mix and the dough thickened to a workable ball. Her floured hands lifted and shaped the dough, then patted it into a circular shape to place in the heated, greased Dutch oven by the outside fire pit. She scooped more coals onto the oven lid and waited. My brother and I stood barefoot on the packed-earth yard, smelling the baking bread, hoping for a taste of the hot pan. She broke off two pieces from the steaming loaf and handed them to us. Maria smiled and we devoured the delicious gift.

Chapter Five

EXPANDED OUTLOOK

Late in the afternoon, Mother, Buzzy, and I went for walks. I remember watching the grasses stirred by subtle breezes and the soft, orange sunlight as it brightened everything it touched like fresh-polished copper. During these gentle times, mother shared stories. Buzzy found rocks and bugs, but I cherished being with her. She told me:

I tried so hard to make a better home here. This house was so old and small that your Daddy and I saw no use spending any more on it than we had to. We had several men over helping to paper and paint and after the paper was all on we were in bed and the thing began to crack all over the house. At first we didn't realize what it was and thought something had caused the guns to go off in the closet under the stairs. It sounded exactly like shooting. But the cheesecloth should have been moistened before the wet wallpaper was put on it and that is what caused the shrinkage and cracking. So all I can say for it is that I know we put new wallpaper on and it is at least clean.

I know that cleanliness was important to Mother. She often complained about the old frame building at Oak Creek saying, "It's hard to clean, Homer." That old house was hard to clean, but even though snakes wandered in under the back door, Mother joked about the house.

"The wind from the cracks in the floor blew my skirt above my head!" We all knew that she was just exaggerating again, but after that, I did notice a current of air on my bare feet when I walked through that room.

Mother and Daddy talked of constructing another house on a flat area overlooking Cattail Falls about a mile south of Oak Creek. From this terrace, you could see the distant falls that poured clear water over the seventy-five foot cliff to the giant stone slabs below. Here, a peaceful pool fed a stream lined with ferns and yellow columbine. The water rippled through gravel and boulders under the shade of gnarled oaks as dragonflies with iridescent wings hovered over the shimmering water.

My parents never built the house at Cattail Falls. Financial problems during the Depression and then the possibility of losing the ranch to a national park left it an unrealized dream. Having to content herself with caring for the old mail-order house at Oak Creek, Mother tried to improve the yard by growing flowers.

You know, Patricia, growing flowers was a production too, with all those rocks in the dirt around the house. I finally talked your father into having some ranch hands haul four loads of dirt and several bags of goat manure from the pens for my flower bed. The old dirt just wouldn't grow anything. We are right here in the bottom of a canyon and the rain washes everything away. We haven't had much rain, but what we had your Daddy called a gully washer. The only way to save dirt was to bank it up with a wall of rocks. That wasn't easy either. I had seven boxes with seedlings. I planted some hollyhock seeds that year and they all came up so beautifully. I made a circle in the side yard, dug it out, and filled it with that good dirt and put rocks around it, but didn't bank it up. We grew zinnias in prune boxes, Patricia, and transplanted them. Remember?

Some of the balsam also came up. I planted carnation seed and stocks and then it rained. I had to stand there and see the water pouring down from the hill in back of the house over my flowerbed and couldn't do a thing. One carnation was tall enough to survive and the water covered everything up with sand right to the top of the zinnias. They were about a foot high so were still growing. Only the flowers and a couple of leaves stuck out after it was all over.

Why did Mother spend so much time trying to grow flowers from seed packets? I knew she teased me and called the whole Oak Creek section her yard. Plenty of flowers grew wild there. The lechuguilla had tall flower stalks like paintbrushes and the prickly pear cactus bore red fruit. I guess she did transplant that beautiful bush from Blue Creek called a yellow trumpet flower, but it didn't grow as well here as it did in the volcanic soil at headquarters. She raved about her night blooming cereus though. One of the men brought it to her. It looked like a scraggly Christmas cactus and grew in the wild in the middle of brush, disguised, and difficult to find. The white bloom looked a little like a waxy lotus blossom in a Japanese painting. Since it only bloomed early in the evening and then for just one night, it seemed a lot of work for little reward. Mother, an exotic flower herself, thought this cactus rare and spectacular.

She told me another story about her early experiences:

I always wanted to go along different places on the ranch. This irritated your father as it made extra work. I wanted to go and camp "On Top" in the mountains. He said: "Well, you'll have to take care of Patricia." You were little then and that meant I either rode up there on Brownie, or I led Brownie and you sat on him. Homer made it as hard as he could. He thought that was something real laughable. I wanted to do something and he made it hard to cure me of wanting to go along.

After many requests, I prevailed and your daddy agreed to take us with him. We spent the first night at headquarters, arose before dawn, packed a mule with overnight camping supplies, and saddled the horses. I used that old army saddle that had a hole in the middle that accommodated my extra tailbone and made riding more comfortable. He rode his white horse as it danced and turned. Homer wore worn chaps over his khakis, a beige canvas jacket, and his usual sweat-stained Stetson. I wore my carpenter's overalls and a sweater. Nights became cooler in the mountains. You wore that little pink suit I knitted with the matching cap.

Mr. Brotherton, who worked on the ranch, went with us. I carried you on a pillow at the front of the saddle. W.D. Smithers, a visiting photographer at Johnson's farm, followed us on a mule. We passed the chimney-like formations of colorful, layered rock in Blue Creek. At the head of Blue Creek, the trail wound up the side of the mountain, switching back and forth to allow the steep climb up the canyon.

We picnicked at the south end of Laguna and then continued our trip to the South Rim. The grass there and on the sides of Blue Creek Canyon grew tall, higher than our horses legs. We passed by pine trees and oaks. Homer pointed out distant mountains, unusual formations, and reddish-brown magma outcroppings. As the land flattened on top of the South Rim, a drop-off of over 2,000 feet, two hawks soared below this escarpment, rising and floating on the updrafts of warm, fall air. White clouds trailed beneath us and above the ridges of mountains and hills below this deep cliff. The magnificent view extended one-hundred miles into old Mexico where mountains there faded to light blue in the distance.

We arrived at Boot Canyon in late afternoon. Our mules and horses picked their way down the rocky trail beneath the weathered column of rock that looked like a cowboy's boot. The soil by the trail turned rich, allowing Douglas Fir, Arizona Cypress, and many grasses to grow along this canyon valley. At Boot Springs, the men unloaded the animals and began making camp. I was just thrilled to death.

Your father intended to make this camp as uncomfortable as possible so I wouldn't want to go along again. He had this tarp and he took pine branches to make me a mattress. Between the layers of pine branches, he placed sharp stones.

The next morning Homer said, "How did you sleep last night, Bergine?"

I told him, "Just wonderful!" I'd been wanting to go up there so much. This kinda took the wind out of his sails and he told me what he did. He showed me the rocks in the pine boughs. I said, "You know, Homer, I didn't feel a one of your rocks. I don't know what happened, but I didn't feel any of them." He was so disappointed that I had a wonderful time. I found out he didn't sleep so well himself on those rocks.

Both my mother and father had wonderful senses of humor. Mother loved to tell funny happenings about the ranch and the people she knew. She even had the ability to tell serious stories in a humorous way. She made people laugh, often relieving tension for all of us.

* * * * *

Whenever Mother was lonely, she walked or rode her horse, Brownie, the two miles to Nail's. My brother sat on a pillow in front of her on the saddle horn. I bounced behind her and held on to the small, leather straps at the back of the saddle. Mother carried a bag of food to share. She said we would have lunch and come back late in the afternoon. I don't know what happened, but Brownie slowed and started stepping sideways when the cinch loosened and the whole saddle went under the horse. I fell off in one direction and Mother with Buzzy dropped on the other side into a patch of lechuguilla. She saw a rattlesnake in the spiny clusters and leaped, dragging my brother to safety. Brownie just stood there, the reins hanging to the ground. After we remounted and arrived at Nail's, Mother told Mr. Nail and Nena about our adventure. "The lucky thing was I wasn't stuck with any of those thorns because they have poison in the points. I didn't have a single puncture, Sam. I just got out of that lechuguilla and we were all right. The snake was as scared as I was and slithered off in another direction."

Mr. Nail cradled the bowl of his pipe in his gnarled hand. His face showed concern. "What about Patricia?"

"I don't know exactly what she did, but she's the kind that takes care of herself. Anyway, she's all right too. We got the horse and I pulled that cinch thing as best I could. Brownie's so tame. He's just an old plug, and he stood there with that snake and everything."

Mr. Nail gripped Brownie's bridle. "Don't ever trust a horse, Bergine, no matter how tame one is, because he can change just like that." He snapped his fingers and looked grim, but Nena and Julia sympathized with us.

Later that afternoon, we rode Brownie home then turned him out to pasture. Saddle tired, we walked to the top of the hill past the gate to watch for my father. Mother sat there on a flat rock while the late afternoon light turned the volcanic rocks and cliffs a terracotta red. The sky glowed like a rainbow as Mother waited and watched for a trail of dust along the main road. When Daddy didn't come home by dusk, we ambled to the house. The shadows of the dark red sides of the Window watched and waited too.

* * * * *

Mother grew in this unlikely place at Oak Creek like the rare blossoms I once found growing in the shadow of three large boulders in Oak Canyon. I felt awe at the beauty of the delicate cream and red blooms, circled and stared at this orchid wonder, then left it to grow untouched. Nearby, a vinegaroon, six-inches long and scorpion-like, scuttled over the damp leaves and hid beneath some logs. His black and brown armor-plating and the smell of vinegar that he ejected made him seem dangerous though the spray was his only defense. This reminded me that beauty and risk coexisted in Big Bend.

My best memory of my mother remained seeing her at her vanity table brushing her long, dark hair until it glistened and shone as it flowed around the stool like a shimmering waterfall. A wood fire crackled in the cast-iron pot-bellied stove. "You need to brush one hundred strokes each day," she admonished me. She pulled hairs from her brush, wound the silky strands around two fingers, and tucked this into her celluloid hair receiver. Then, she polished her nails with a chamois buffer. In the mirror's reflection, she looked like a Madonna from an old painting with hair parted in the middle, large, soulful eyes, and a Mona Lisa smile.

My father recognized Mother's special qualities. However, because of Mother's early blunders in Big Bend, whenever Daddy left us, he always turned to me and said, "Take care of your mother, Patricia. Remember, she's a city girl."

Chapter Six

SEEING A BETTER LIFE

When my father first came to the Big Bend, he found a
family of bandits camped at the head of Blue Creek.
Since Pancho Villa's men had raided the southern part of
this area in the past, many ranchers feared bandit activity.
As a result of the stories told about these raids, Daddy
approached a family of outlaws named Baiza camped on his
land by Cedar Spring in upper Blue Creek canyon. My
father's white horse snorted as he drew back on the reins.
Fog spilled from the mountains, dampening the oak leaves.
Daddy's hand dropped to his rifle in its leather case by his
saddle. His workman on a mule also carried a gun.
Mournful sounds of the doves joined the buzz and clicks of
insects.

The desperados stood their ground by the campsite. They
wore stained, white pants and shirts with leather-thong sandals, the soles cut from old automobile tires. Wide-brimmed
straw hats caught an occasional drip from the trees. Several
rifles and bands of bullets leaned on tree trunks near their
bedrolls. The moment seemed frozen except the lazy cir-

cling smoke movement. The black, dented coffee pot hissed and the smell of baking bread in the Dutch oven filled the campsite. One bandit choked, "Candelario!"

My father edged his horse toward the bandit leader who glared and dropped his hands closer to the pistols at his belt. They spoke in clipped Spanish. The outlaw punctuated the air with his calloused hands.

Daddy urged the horse forward several steps, the metal shoes clipped the stone slabs of the trail sending clanking echoes down the canyon. "You must leave now!"

Candelário Baiza grimaced. *"Por qué, Señor?"*

"Why? Because you are camped on my ranch and you cannot stay here!" Cold feelings of silent fear gripped my father, but his face stayed calm.

"No entiendo, Señor."

"You do understand. If you don't leave now, I will throw you off the ranch!"

The outlaws stared. Candelario's dark eyes narrowed, then he shrugged and motioned his gang to gather the bedding and supplies before they rode down the Blue Creek mountainside the seventeen miles toward the Rio Grande and Mexico.

Mother experienced a similar problem. When I was a baby in 1931, she did sit-up exercises on the downstairs bedroom floor. She raised herself and saw a strange Mexican man looking in the window. He gestured and waved his arms, the tattered sleeves hung streaked and dirty. Mother could not understand what this man wanted. She threw on her jacket and met him at the porch steps. Since she didn't speak Spanish and he spoke no English, all she knew was his frantic body language. Finally, the hired man came and explained in broken English that the stranger fled bandits who chased him from Mexico across the ranch. At this point, Mother sent the workman for my father at Blue Creek.

The bedraggled Mexican told my father pursuers planned to hang him. Daddy and other Big Bend men formed a posse and rode into Mexico after the outlaws. Ranchers had little help from law enforcement in those days, forcing the ranchers to settle many differences themselves. I never heard what happened in Mexico. However, that was the last of our outlaw troubles. As a result of this incident, a long relationship began with the stranger, José Arias, who worked with us for many years.

I asked Julia if she knew any bandit stories, and she told me about her father, Sam Nail, and the Glenn Springs raid:

> On May 5, 1916, my father started to Glenn Springs from his ranch at Burro Mesa. He stopped at Burnham's place and asked Gid Hubbard, one of Mother's cousins, if he wanted to go also. Gid said he had a job to do, but if Sam waited until the next day, he did want to go. When they arrived at Glenn Springs, the terrible raid was over and there were looters everywhere. Asked about this incident, my father said he "killed two dogs and shot a hole through a woman's hat." That's all I ever heard him say about the incident. Since Daddy was a good story teller, I never knew how much to believe. Others, such as Mr. Wade, who rode to help after the raid, said Daddy's pipe bowl was shot out of his mouth. He thought my father looked humorous riding and clenching his pipe stem with his teeth. If Daddy's pipe was shot off of the stem, then I would say there was probably quite a bit of truth to the story!

Sam and Gid missed the Glenn Springs Raid by one day. On May 5, 1916, Mexican residents in the little community of Glenn Springs celebrated Cinco de Mayo with friends from both sides of the Rio Grande. At 11:00P.M. that night a band of bandits from Mexico surprised the town. Two of the nine soldiers of the Fourteenth Infantry had guard duty. The others rested in tents. Many villagers slept at this time. When the outlaws began shooting, the soldiers fled into an adobe building for protection. The desperados fired the thatch roof and it fell on the soldiers. Three of them died from gunshot wounds and another received dangerous wounds. The rest had painful burns. Though numerous residents received injuries, only one child perished in the gunfire. The bandits gathered their dead and wounded, then rode for Boquillas. There they robbed the Deemer store.

Julia said the unease along the border lasted for many years. "It took some time for people to learn to trust their Mexican neighbors again. My father had a horse and saddle stolen during this time. Ranchers always left their houses unlocked because if they were gone and someone came along, this person was sure to be hungry and tired, so it was unthinkable to lock him out. The visitor would go in, cook a meal, and probably spend the night before going on his way."

Elinor Cartledge Howie, daughter of Robert Cartledge of Terlingua and niece of Wayne Cartledge of Castolon, told me about a similar incident:

> We were heading for school outside the Big Bend when we stopped for flooding. We went down to cross Terlingua Creek toward Castolon when the other crossings were impassable. Daddy got safely across, then Mother in her Buick sedan, and then the mail truck. It took us longer to get across Terlingua Creek and over the road to the mountains than anticipated, so Mother hadn't made a lunch. She and the mail-truck driver decided to stop at the Waddy Burnham ranch to eat. We did that, but no one was home. So, we fixed lunch, cleaned up, and went on to Marathon leaving a "thank you" for the Burnhams.

* * * * *

My father established his headquarters five miles down

Blue Creek from the outlaw encampment in the first year of ranching in the Chisos. This center of activity lay in a small valley below Signal Peak. Shrub greasewood grew on the valley floor with gravel and tumbled rocks piled from when Blue Creek flooded in ancient times. Sedimentary limestone, shale, and different clays, pushed and tortured by long-ago volcanic activity, left colored rocks and strange yet beautiful stacked formations. Sotol, with its clusters of slender, saw-toothed leaves grew over the magma-covered hills. The view from these surroundings included the blue Mesa de Anguilla of Mexico, cut by the darker shadow of Santa Elena Canyon.

Daddy focused on roads to and from headquarters as one of the first building activities on the ranch. Workers scraped and dug the road from Nail's the three miles to the shearing pens. A portion of this road followed a creek bed. Roads usually followed old trails, paths, and gravel washes, often the easiest way from one place to another. My father enlarged these paths into narrow roads. From the pens to Blue Creek, he blasted sections of road from solid limestone using dynamite. This road, wide enough for one vehicle, wound over hills and down arroyos to the top of the ridge above the headquarters site. Again, he dynamited the road to the bottom of the ridge. This narrow portion tipped slightly to the downside giving a feeling of sliding off to tumble the several hundred feet to the valley.

Driving these primitive roads caused anxiety and fear for any novice like Mother. She told me about her driving experiences in Big Bend:

> When I first visited Big Bend in my Essex car, it went out of control south of Persimmon Gap. I had driven before, but I had this accident with my car. I left it up there near Cooper's store and when Homer went back, all the wheels had been stolen. What happened to me was I lost the radius rod. That means your front wheels go every which

way. There was no control over the car. I just went off the road and up in a sotol bush which was lucky for me. Then I walked to Cooper's and he took me to the ranch. So, I just didn't want to drive anymore.

Daddy determined to teach Mother to drive on the ranch roads, a terrible place to conquer fear. She resisted. "Driving is bad enough; driving on these ranch roads is impossible."

Daddy lectured, "You have to know how to drive in this country, Bergine. What if something happens to me? You have to do this."

They began on the clay and gravel road from Oak Creek to Blue Creek.

Mother did all right until they passed the vast shearing pens and started up the first rocky ridge where Daddy had blasted the narrow road from the side of the bluff. Sheer rock bordered the right side of the car and a drop-off of several hundred feet crowded the left.

Mother leaned forward and gripped the steering wheel with both hands. Sweat shimmered on her face and neck as she crept up the hill. One mile farther she braked for the road down the Blue Creek ridge. Several goats wandered across the road as the car crept forward, pushing close to the hillside. Loose rock clattered and tumbled to the valley. This tortuous path ended at the gravel plain and the headquarters house. After this, she drove in Big Bend without complaining.

Daddy's good friend, Dr. Lockhart of Alpine, did protest when he visited us at Blue Creek. "You need to fix the road down that hill, Homer. It's terrible!"

My father chuckled. "It's just the way I want it, Bill. We see the Border Patrol men coming to the ranch and have plenty of time before they get here."

Labor did present another serious problem in our isolated, tough country. Few workers came from Alpine, 126 miles away, or Marathon, eighty-six miles distant. Many laborers lived near the Rio Grande in Big Bend or just across the river in Mexico. Most of these spoke Spanish. We called them Mexicans, but not with any derogatory meaning. A large number of our seven to twenty-four hired hands lived north of the Rio Grande.

Occasionally, women appeared on the payroll. Clara Hannold worked during roundup and shearing in the summer of 1936. Lott Felts had his daughter, Lunetta, camp in the mountainous area at Laguna where she herded Angora goats. Mrs. Felts cooked and kept books. I don't remember very many women on the ranch, as my father preferred hiring single men when possible.

When we needed extra help we called on Chata, Mrs. Juan Sada. This cultured, attractive lady and her husband ran a store and café at Boquillas some twenty-seven miles east of Oak Canyon. Infrequently, Daddy asked if we wanted dinner at Chata's. Of course Mother and I were thrilled at this idea knowing this meant a Mexican meal. Buzzy smiled also, though I'm not sure he knew much about the plans as he wobbled to join the family.

The International truck bumped past Burnham's ranch below Green Gulch along the foothills of the Chisos to Boquillas, a tiny town near the Rio Grande. The Sierra Del Carmen mountain range with its layers of rock turning pale pink in the late afternoon sun loomed nearby. Chata's adobe café had a brush arbor with a dirt floor. She met us at the door then guided us to the small tables. The spicy smell of chili, frijole beans, and cooked tomatoes filled the room.

"Quiere comer, Señor?"

"Sí. We plan to eat, Chata." My father tipped his hat with respect.

"Cuántos?" The lamp light caught the gray streaks in her hair like a halo.

"Ocho, Chata. Eight." We sat at a painted wooden table near a window. A cheerful, multicolored woven rug hung on the nearest wall. Through the opening we viewed the tops of giant cane and the caliche hills below the majestic

Sierra del Carmen mountain range.

How strange! Our four people didn't make eight for dinner. I didn't know at the time that Chata had sent word to the Mexican town across the Rio Grande, also called Boquillas, for four ranch workers. After our delicious meal of tacos and enchiladas, we climbed in the truck cab and headed home.

A full moon lit the countryside as we jostled toward the Chisos. Stars filled the blue sky, glimmering above the purple mountains. A lone jackrabbit froze in the headlights then loped beneath a mesquite bush. Its eyes reflected light like candles in the night. When we turned onto our road at the mailbox, the dark shadow of the Window's silhouette stood guard.

After Daddy parked beneath the oak trees near the wall, the tarp in the truck bed moved, then lifted. Four Mexican men, called "wetbacks," or "illegals," by the Border Patrol, climbed down and unloaded their bedrolls. This answered the mystery of the strange number Daddy gave Chata at dinner. Later, Daddy told Mother he never solved his labor problems in Big Bend:

> It is so hard to get responsible men. When I first drove sheep to the ranch, the herders let the animals escape. It takes ten years to learn to work sheep. I feared they would scatter them all over Brewster County. Now, labor's main object is to get by without doing anything. If things don't change at the ranch, I am going to run the whole outfit off and start over.

With close family, my father felt free to vent his frustration in brief complaints. With other people, Wilson tradition held that a person didn't burden others with their problems. To other people, he seemed calm and collected most of the time. Mother called this an example of the stoic man of the West: strong, brave, and quiet.

Chapter Seven

BEYOND THE WINDOW

The headquarters site lacked water. Sixteen distant springs including Oak, Cherry, Boot, Cedar, Ward, Burro, Tule, Wasp, and Mule Ear with seven smaller springs gave some water for animals, but did not help workers at headquarters. At first they hauled what they needed to Blue Creek and lived in tents while installing pipelines, troughs, and tanks. On November 2, 1929, Daddy wrote to Mother:

> I am so frustrated! A five-mile pipeline was put in. I instructed them how to put air vents on all high topography. They just ignored my telling them about the air vents and now the line has to be cut in about twenty places and tees put in for air vents, I have put up with their bum work as long as I can. If I am not present they pull off something every day that costs me a lot of money.

In order to push water uphill and solve the Blue Creek water-hauling problem, my father used his surface-water pump that he patented August 13, 1929, on the windmill at the shearing pens below Ward Mountain. This mechanism of metal pipes and valves worked by pushing the water a short way, then other valves kept that liquid from flowing backwards. Eventually the pipes brought the forced water over hills much higher than the windmill containing the pump. This device allowed him to pipe water the two miles over hills to headquarters without electricity. The pump also filled other tanks and troughs on his ranch. He installed one of his pumps for his neighbor, Sam Nail, attaching the device to the windmill near his house, enabling Mr. Nail to drive water to the top of Burro Mesa for his cattle.

Headers, earthen dams built at the head of gullies to form small ponds, gave another solution for watering wildlife and livestock. I remember climbing the side of an arroyo to its source up Ward Mountain. Here my father and the foreman stood by a half-finished dam discussing its progress. Two workmen dug and shoveled rocks and soil on to the bank. The beige and brown dirt sprayed as it plunked on the barrier. I smelled the dust and pungent odors of cut roots with the clicking of tools against stones. As I looked past the Mexican persimmon bush, I saw the valley of the shearing pens. Even a mile away, I could still hear the distant clank of the windmill.

* * * * *

During 1929 and 1930 while my father purchased and consolidated his land, workers concentrated on fencing the different pastures with woven wire for an Angora goat and Rambouillet sheep operation. One of his goals was rotating stock to prevent land damage. He used care in how many animals he put in a pasture also. He said to me, "If you damage the land, it ruins your livelihood."

Before he enclosed his ranch with woven-wire fencing, animals roamed free with only a few drift fences to turn livestock on the Wilson holdings. My father was the first to fence his area with woven wire. None of the adjoining landowners complained. They seemed to view this fencing as my father keeping his sheep and goats off their land. Sam Nail enclosed his land with strands of barbed wire, a practice followed by most area cattle ranchers by the mid-1930s.

Our neighbor, Sam Nail, chuckled about his friend's fences and said, "Homer, I could ride all the way to the river without stopping for wire before you built your fences, twenty miles each way, to see about lost cattle and horses. I didn't bother with food or water, just ate along the way when I stopped to ask about lost stock. Sometimes I had to sleep on my saddle blanket. When it got cold, I'd fire a sotol bush."

Daddy and his ranch neighbor to the southwest, Wayne Cartledge, paid for the border fence between their ranches. This woven-wire barrier attached to cedar posts went from the South Rim toward the river then turned near Castolon to go northwest to Tule Mountain and finally east to Burro Mesa, enclosing our largest pasture of sixteen sections. Within the Wilson ranch, cross fences broke the land into grazing grounds varying in size from half-section traps to large enclosures. Each pasture contained at least one water source.

One of my earliest memories focused on going with my father to camp out at the Chimneys, tall red and brown layered stacks of stone worn into fantastic shapes by wind and water. They looked like prehistoric monsters guarding the lower part of Blue Creek. We jostled down the sand and gravel of the creek bed past Wasp, Burro, and Tule springs and around the foot of Kit Mountain. As Daddy drove, he pointed out rock formations and explained erosion. Workmen unloaded some fencing supplies while I explored the Chimneys.

That night, after a supper of Vienna Sausage and crackers with cool water from the canvas bag hanging on the truck, we slept on old army cots of wood and canvas. We looked at the dark blue sky, a bowl of stars that seemed close enough to touch. Daddy pointed to the North Star and the Big Dipper, opening a world of wonder to me. I went to sleep with the sounds of a coyote howling near Castolon.

The next day the fencing continued. My father also used natural barriers such as the high bluff at Burro Mesa as part of an enclosure. Workers then dug holes for the cedar posts with shovels and post-hole diggers. In places, picks and crowbars pried and removed large stones and saws cut low-growing brush during the tedious work. An old truck hauled more posts and wire across Blue Creek and over the lechuguilla and greasewood-covered hills to Burro Mesa where he used the high bluff as part of the enclosure.

Later, the old truck lurched and whined the five miles up Blue Creek where men unloaded and piled more cedar logs in cross layers. The remnants of bark covered the truck bed as the clean, cedar smell drifted in the cold, winter air. Many places proved too rough and difficult for a truck to pass. Mules then pulled posts and wire, and hands carried it up the sides of mountains.

Fencing left openings as it crossed gullies and arroyos where coyotes and other predators crawled under the wire. To prevent this, the men attached sections of woven wire to the bottom of the fence line and weighted this extra mesh with large stones. When water gushed through the creek bed after an infrequent storm, the water gap washed free saving the main fence.

Re-building enclosures continued through all the years at the ranch. Our foreman in 1932, Herbert Wright, wrote to my father about the problems with contracted fence building on the southwest part of the ranch.

Homer, I went over to the fence, the Tule fence. I rode the line, and on the east side going west there are 23 rolls of wire up, about half of it aproned. Down the first big draw is where he put the first gate. He used all the little lineposts for the corners but used the 2 good posts for the gate.

The best I could tell there are 20 or 30 loose posts. The posts measure up about 10, 11, 13, feet

The Pour Off at the Window.

Homer Wilson.

Bergine Wilson.

Patricia at Oak Creek, 1932.

Ada Johnson holding Patricia at Johnsons, June 16, 1932.

Bergine and Patricia at Oak Creek.

Julia Nail holding Patricia, 1933.

Mail-order house at Oak Creek.

Patricia on a hill behind the mail-order house at Oak Creek.

Homer, Bergine, and Patricia on the South Rim.

Sam Nail as a young man.

Nena Burnham (Nail) as a young woman.

Patricia and her pet deer at Oak Creek.

Patricia and Homer Jr. in front of Mexican house at Oak Creek.

Homer, Bergine, and Patricia "On Top," 1932.

Chisos Mountains spring.

Patricia on the South Rim.

Sears Roebuck mail-order house at Oak Creek.

Homer, Bergine, and Patricia
at a spring near Marathon.

Camping at Blue Creek, 1935.
Julia Nail (front left) Waddy Burnham (behind Julia),
Bergine Wilson (center) holding Patricia (in bonnet).

Visitors at Oak Creek.

Patricia and Bergine at Cattail Falls.

apart, (by steps). If you remember that the wire stretches up to the old road where it turns to go up the hill, counting from there, there are 124 posts from there to the top of the hill. There are several posts out on that line that's not in. And from the top of the hill going down west there's about ½ or ¾ of a mile where there has been no posts set.

Homer, it does not look like much of a fence to me. It's all in a mess. Oh yes, the other gate is west of the mountain right at the foot of the hill — not where you wanted it.

Mr. Wright and my father had serious problems with this fence builder. Though the man declared the pasture fence all right when he finished, within three days time, 300 sheep escaped. Daddy told Mother he had put up with shoddy work as long as he could.

Eventually, my father enclosed the home place with sheep-proof fence to keep the goats out of the living area at Oak Creek. The curious meat goats would climb everything including our car and truck, where their sharp hooves dented and scratched the metal and paint. They also ate the newly planted flowers, which made them very unpopular with Mother.

*   *   *   *   *

In the early days before he married and after Daddy had fenced some pastures, he stocked his land. He shipped over 4,000 fine-wooled Rambouillet sheep from north of Comstock in early October of 1929, unloading west of Sanderson. Workers on horseback drove them the remaining one hundred miles across the Cox place to his ranch in Big Bend.

In a letter to Mother, he said:

During the holidays I bought 3,500 head of Angora

goats that I will ship down on the 17th. I don't believe this bunch will cause us much grief as the weather is ideal for moving them now.

On February 2, 1930, he wrote:

In moving those goats down I wrote you about buying, we encountered the coldest weather of the year. It was just five degrees above zero when we unloaded them at 5A.M. in Marathon. How would you like to camp out during such weather? It was nearly that cold several nights while we were on the road.

* * * * *

It seemed that someone was building something at all times. Mother claimed Daddy spent everything he made on improvements. As soon as possible, the men built a one-room concrete house and a smaller rock building to replace the tents at Blue Creek. Wire took the place of the poles stuck in the ground for temporary pens and an open-air shed with a roof of sotol poles thatched with greasewood served now as a ramada, a brush arbor, a shaded place for shoeing horses and doing forge work at headquarters.

Before my father built the new house at Headquarters, he decided to construct a concrete and stone holding tank for water at the top of the ridge just north of the small concrete house. It took several days with three workmen shoveling, making forms, and pouring the mix to complete the project. Now the water from the surface-water pump on the windmill at the shearing pens poured into this new tank to gather pressure for the new house.

Mother wanted a larger house built at Blue Creek as a place to stay when we went to headquarters and for more space for the foreman and his family. My father agreed. She dreamed of building the place with materials "off the land."

Many houses in Big Bend, including the Nails' home, used this concept.

With the additional leased sections from Wayne Cartledge, taking the ranch close to the Rio Grande, laborers found most of the materials Mother wanted on the ranch. Mules dragged pine logs from Boot Canyon down the mountains for ceiling beams. Workers cut cane from the banks of the Rio Grande to cover these timbers. Over this cane the builder spread a layer of concrete mixed with gravel for a more substantial ceiling than the usual mud over cane. Raphael Acosta, the builder, left an air space of about eight inches for airflow before he roofed the building with tin. Large flagstones from Blue Creek floored the concrete and stone building. The plan for the house included two bedrooms, a living room, kitchen with a dining area, and a long screened-in porch. Knotty-pine partitions separated the rooms. The divider by the dining area created an open office for a desk, map-making supplies, and ranch papers.

A long, pine table stood on the flagstone floor east of the kitchen covered with red-checkered oilcloth. I don't remember a bug problem other than an occasional fly that came in through the screen door. However, I do know the legs of this table stood in partially-filled cans of water to keep insects and ants from crawling onto the table top.

Single and double beds lined the side of the building on the screened porch. We sat on three sides of the porch on a built-in wall. A large, covered container rested in the corner by the screen door where the canvas water bag hung. Inside this crock floated slabs of clear, golden honeycomb. I loved to carry a chunk of dripping wax to the back steps, lick the sticky syrup, and chew the comb like gum. I saw this as the good life.

Seeing a better life and working to make this a reality took most of my father's time. He viewed harnessing nature as a positive good. If he fell from a horse, he mounted again, finished his job, and rode to success within view of the Window.

Chapter Eight

CONNECTED VIEWS

While my father continued building the Wilson ranch, Mother, Buzzy, and I spent most of our time at Oak Canyon. On a March day in 1937, the hired man rode fence, so Mother had to catch Brownie herself. This contrary horse slunk away from her in the pasture, then trotted up a hill and turned as if to tell her she could not reach him. Finally, Mother threw the bridle over her shoulder and trudged home.

That day we walked to Nail's, stopping to rest now and then to enjoy the perfect spring day. Since Mother went at a slow pace for Buzzy's sake, this gave me time to enjoy nature. I scanned for interesting things like pretty rocks and unusual insects. If it moved, it got my attention. I saw an alligator lizard scurry over gray rocks and under a clump of mesquite, its blue-gray stripes like jagged lines on the darker body. Further on, a covey of quail whirred and flew from the brush by the road.

When we arrived, another car was parked near the front of the adobe. Sam and Mr. Davenport from the Basin above the Window visited as they walked from Sam's milo field to the tree near the steps. Sam liked to grow things and had raised alfalfa and frijole beans irrigated from his stock tank until the tank filled with silt, making irrigation impractical. The Nails also had a large vegetable garden with radishes, carrots, onions, tomatoes, squash, green beans, cantaloupes, watermelon, peppers, cabbage, and turnips. Cicadas hummed and birds sang in the trees as Mother and Mrs. Nail talked of raising flowers.

I leaned against Julia, home for the weekend from school in Marathon. Sam and Mr. Davenport climbed into his vehicle and started from the house. I looked down at Sam's metal washpan filled with tomato plants that had been grown in soil and were now ready for transplanting.

Suddenly, Nena and Mother screamed as my little brother toddled behind the car then slipped and fell beneath the back wheel. I stared as time hung in the air like a single slide on a movie scene. It seemed I couldn't breathe as we ran toward Buzzy lying still on the ground.

Mother cradled my injured brother on her lap as Mr. Davenport raced us to the first-aid station at the Civilian Conservation Corps in the Basin. When they couldn't help, he urged his vehicle over the dusty roads to Alpine. Buzzy suffered, whimpered, and cried as we bumped along with Mother holding him and patting his broken bones.

We arrived at Annie Kate Ferguson's house. Alpine didn't have a hospital then. This good friend summoned a doctor as Mother carried Homer Jr. to a bedroom. The tire had crushed all the bones on the right side of his chest and slid over part of his head, leaving faint tread marks at his temple. For two weeks we stayed with Annie Kate, wondering if my brother would live. Weeks later, his young body did mend, and he survived his injuries.

At the time of the accident, Homer Jr. walked, ran, and spoke in short sentences. After his recovery, he learned again to walk and talk. For several years, one of his feet dragged to the side. The accident also impaired his speech for a year. Finally, he healed with no remaining handicaps. When Homer Jr. improved enough to travel home, Daddy drove us in the old Hupmobile. My brother sat with Mother in the back seat, and I sat up front with Daddy, which allowed me to see more through the front and side windows. Antelope grazed between Alpine and Marathon that morning as the early light misted the grasslands. One pronghorn flicked his tail, chewed, and stared as we passed, the beige and white of his coat a tapestry against the greening spring grasses.

As we crossed Tornillo Creek and turned below the mountains near the Burnham's land, my father told Mother, "We need to stop at Burnham's, Bergine. Waddy's worried about the national park talk, and I told him I'd let him know what I heard in Alpine. Most seemed excited about the whole thing. I guess they're careful not to say much, since we may lose our land over this whole thing. Many appeared to favor the idea, though."

"That's what I heard too," Mother replied, "The people there think it'll bring business to the area, but I didn't think the state settled the money problem. It's so undecided and frustrating. No wonder Waddy worries. I know his wife does too."

The Burnham ranch bordered the road, their house visible at Government Springs. Lavender-pink verbena bloomed on the graded shoulders like bright paint splashed from an artist's brush. The craggy Chisos loomed above us where we turned onto the dirt road at Waddy and Dessie Ferol Burnham's place. I watched as a hawk circled and floated below the white clouds hunting its prey.

Julia said two houses stood there at the foot of Green Gulch when her mother's family first came to Big Bend. The smaller house rested close to the spring. The other house, situated about a quarter of a mile away on the top of a hill and originally a two-room building made of sticks and mud, now had five new lumber rooms (three bedrooms, a dining room, and a kitchen) and a front and a back porch.

It's strange the things I remember about the Burnham home, such as the one room papered with covers from magazines. I thought about my brother's accident. Serious accidents happened to our neighbors also. Most ranch families lost at least one child when the youngster fell from a horse or the animal dragged him when his foot entangled in the stirrup. Charlie Burnam, Sam's brother-in-law, had most of the bones in his body broken from ranch-work mishaps. Nena's brother, Waddy, had several problems too.

Waddy left his horse at the top of a canyon one day, then walked, looking for one of his cows. His boot slipped on a little water, and he fell into the deep ravine, breaking his leg. He lay trapped at the rocky bottom until several men found him and pulled him out of the chasm with ropes.

Another time, a cow hooked out Waddy's eye. It hung on his cheek as his family covered the injured eyeball and then carried him to safety. They placed him in the wagon bed and started to Marathon for help. After a ten-hour trip bumping and lurching through gullies and arroyos, they arrived in town, where Dr. Worthington put the eyeball back in its socket, and saved his vision.

Julia never tired of my questions about our neighbors — most of them were her relatives, though I never grasped all of these relationships. She understood my interest in the people and ways, so she humored me. Actually, I trusted her and liked to hear her share stories of the people and the past. I recognized her caring and patience.

My attention returned to the Burnhams as we parked at the wooden porch. Waddy and his sons, Waddy T. III and Bill, strolled toward the car. Mrs. Burnham and the boys, home for the weekend from school at Marathon where she taught and kept discipline without seeming to try, waved from the porch. Her strong personality did not show as she kept order and got her way in a quiet manner at home and at school.

Waddy, brother of Nena Nail and grandson of Captain Jesse Burnham who came to Texas with Stephen F. Austin's first colony, looked the part of a pioneer rancher. His long-sleeved cotton shirt opened at the neck and leather chaps hung low from his waist with large pockets to the sides. As he approached, his rolled-brimmed Stetson tipped forward, casting a shadow on his pointed nose and chin, which seemed to jut forward giving him a determined look. His friendly smile greeted us. "Sorry about Buzzy's accident. Glad he's better. We want to help any way and any time we can, Bergine."

Mother carried Buzzy, and we left the men to visit on the wooden porch. Julia's Aunt Ferol greeted us. After murmurs and comments on my brother's ordeal, and lemonade with sugar cookies, I left to wander in the yard, an oasis with a garden, fruit trees, and dewberry vines. The fruit trees, loaded with pink and white blossoms, attracted bees. A gentle breeze carried their buzz with the rustle of the branches as loose petals floated to the ground like light snowflakes. The horse trough filled with clear, cold spring water, reflected my yellow hair and brown eyes as I leaned to watch a catfish swimming lazily, put there after a fishing trip to the river near Castolon.

Julia told me her mother and the other Burnham girls rode sidesaddle when they first came here. Their father insisted the girls ride astride as he thought riding sidesaddle dangerous in this country of sharp rocks and poisonous snakes. The girls wore lovely riding outfits, like culottes, that their mother had made them. These ankle-length skirts with a button-down panel in front hid the skirt division. Unbuttoned, the attractive, parted clothing made safe, riding attire. In my mind I saw these lovely young women trotting across the hills. They wore high-collared blouses with puffed sleeves and jaunty, dark hats on their rolled hair. Gloves protected their hands from the sun, a necessity in those days.

When we left our neighbor's house, I carried the fresh-baked fruit pie Mrs. Burnham gave us, a token of concern and compassion for our ordeal. The warm aroma of berries and spices drifted as we bumped and dipped the twelve miles to Oak Creek.

The next day, the Nails came to visit, and Nena brought my brother's favorite chocolate cake. He loved this attention. They also gave him a little metal car. He grinned as he clutched the toy with his good arm. His perky blue eyes crinkled and his little ears poked through sandy-colored hair. Mother placed him in the shade by the front porch where he pushed his new automobile in the dirt. Dusty lounged by the front steps as if protecting Buzzy.

Mrs. Nail asked about Mother's quilt and the crocheted bedspread, her latest projects. The quilt top, appliquéd with a flower pattern of blues, pinks, and whites, hung in the quilting frame in the west bedroom upstairs. My mother prided herself on the tiny stitches made by pushing the needle straight up then down through the material and padding. She planned to enter the quilt at the Marfa fair. The bedspread of white contained raised nubs. She crocheted in a square pattern then joined the blocks, planning to add fringe later. Mother and Nena shared a love for handwork.

"Beautiful stitching, Bergine. You're almost finished with the quilt. The bedspread is coming along too. Good for you!" Nena gazed at Mother, with a gentle and thoughtful look. They continued talk of stitches, colors, materials, and patterns.

Mother turned to Julia: "That's it by the window. I brought that trunk when we first came to Marathon and stayed at the Gage Hotel. Let me tell you that story."

> Homer insisted that I store it at our room there, as I wouldn't wear good clothes on the ranch. I hated to leave the filmy dinner gowns, high-heeled shoes with cut-steel buckles, embroidered blouses, silk pajamas, and ribbon-trimmed undergarments. When Homer and I returned from the ranch, one of the ladies of Marathon exclaimed about the

lovely clothes I had in the trunk. Can you imagine? A group of women opened it to look at my things while I was gone. I was horrified. Anyway, I store those clothes and a few mementos here for Patricia. Someday she will enjoy things from the twenties.

Julia and I left Mother and Mrs. Nail. As we went downstairs, Julia told me how much it meant to her mother to have a good friend. When my mother first came to the ranch in 1930, Mrs. Nail still grieved for their nine-year-old son, Bob, who died in 1928 from complications following measles. Julia felt this sorrow drew her mother and my mother closer and created a bond as they both suffered losses. Years later, she told me, "Bergine was very understanding, and Mother appreciated this. Although I missed Bob very much, I knew my parents were devastated by his death. They managed to keep from me this great distress, and I have always been grateful to them for this. They were taught to not show their emotions."

We passed through the screened porch. Daddy and Mr. Nail didn't appear to notice us as they talked about the possible park.

"You're right, Homer. Waddy agonizes over this national park thing. I don't know what will happen. We spend our lives improving our places. Now, we may lose everything."

"All we can do right now, Sam, is wait. I don't want to borrow trouble. Maybe they won't raise the money."

Julia and I decided to hunt for arrowheads on the hill above the house while our parents visited. Although she was almost sixteen, she seemed like my close friend, not an adult. I pointed out the Indian grinding stone called a metate, its worn-down depression evidence of this flat place as a campground. Long ago some Mescalero Apaches, and Basket Maker Indians before them, ground seeds, mesquite beans, and maize on this stone. When they left, the heavy rectangular rock stayed.

We walked back and forth, as our eyes searched the rocky ground for chipped flint. We found a few broken arrow-heads, but no perfect keepers here. I kept a little box for my finds by my cot on the porch. Julia had a larger collection, some of them tiny arrowheads for hunting birds.

Mrs. Nail and Julia loved to hunt rocks at their place. They walked in the hills and picked up whatever struck their fancy. An old Indian campground close to their home supplied some arrowheads and a few brightly colored chips of flint. Julia joked she carried a ton of rocks to the house from the surrounding hills and flats. She said her mother had a very good eye for finding the very tiny arrowheads that she walked right over. Someone in Mrs. Nail's family found a small, red pictograph of a buffalo. Nena had a museum-quality, hinged shell fossil from the flats, but Sam gave it to a visiting researcher. If someone wanted something, Mr. Nail hated to refuse him, though hurt feelings in the family might follow.

A number of potholes, another version of a grinding place, filled an exposed area of limestone by Oak Creek not far from the pens. The dark, deep holes looked like donut cutouts on a floured breadboard. Many of the cavities filled with sand and gravel when the creek flooded. Other times the rushing waters exposed more deep depressions, reminders of the Indians camping long ago. I imagined the mysterious sounds of voices bouncing back from the bluffs by the Window like whispers from the past.

I told Julia about the mounds on the hill behind the Mexican house, but she didn't know what they might be either. My grandfather from St. Louis dug in one hill when he visited, but found nothing. He surmised the hills of rock and brush-covered dirt as Indian burial places. The lives of these early dwellers who came to Oak Canyon remained a mystery.

As we hunted, Julia told me more about her family. She said her father and his brother, Jim, came to Brewster County in 1909. They first lived near Dugout. Later, they built a log cabin in Pine Canyon, called Nail Canyon then. They moved to the west side of the Chisos in about 1916 where they constructed their two-room adobe house, later adding another room and a porch.

The Nail brothers, famous walkers, often threw their satchels on the mail hack as it passed, then started hiking ahead of the coach. Many times the walking Nail brothers beat the mail to Alpine, a trip of over ninety miles. Jim Nail married and lived in Alpine leaving the house below Burro Mesa for Sam.

Sam married Nena Burnham in 1918 at her mother's home in Marathon. They went from there to Burro Mesa in a surrey drawn by mules. Fringe around the top swayed as Nena carried her belongings, including her piano, to begin their new life. Julia's brother Bob arrived in 1919 and she followed in 1921.

Most of the Nail twenty-two section ranch lay on the top of Burro Mesa. Many small springs furnished enough water for their cattle. When Sam first came to Brewster County, he brought Black Angus cattle. He felt them less susceptible to pink eye and black leg than the white-faced cattle. However, since he could not ship a carload of calves at one time, he had to conform to the local practices. Everyone raised Herefords at that time. Buyers wanted uniformity in a carload of stock.

The neighboring ranchers got together when it came time to sell the calves. They helped each other work cattle, brand, and get a herd to drive to Marathon to the stockyards where the cattle would be taken by rail to feedlots or packing houses.

Julia finished her story:

> I can't remember the last time a herd was driven to town. It would have been up until the time that the highway department began to work the road and I believe even after that because I remember Mr. Bond was with us. He drove the chuck wagon and

cooked for the drive. This would have been 1931 or 1932. Before that, trucks could not get over the road. The cattle drive would take about a week.

I saw Mr. Nail in my mind riding with the cattle, slapping his coiled rope against his chaps as they drove the animals through mesquite and cactus by Slickrock to the mine road by the O2 ranch. Clouds of dust blew across the red and white cattle and whirled over the men. They stopped for water at Peña Colorado, the old Cavalry Post built to protect Big Bend from bandits. Cottonwoods lined the clear stream making another oasis in the Marathon Basin. The mountains to the south seemed a jagged, blue line on the horizon.

Seeing visions of ranch work seemed exciting, but I liked to imagine Sam making things for Julia. He built a cradle for her out of sotol poles, like other cribs except its sides did not lift down. The rope bottom crisscrossed like some old cots. Once, Julia showed it to me. She told me recently that she would give anything if they had kept the cradle, but it finally fell apart.

Sam also built a Christmas tree with a sotol pole as a trunk. He drilled holes in the stalk where branches of cedar fit, making it look like a real tree. After Christmas, Mrs. Nail dismantled and stored the base and pole with ease.

Most of us in Big Bend found and used a small pine from Green Gulch for our holiday celebration. It took a full afternoon to find a little tree, cut and haul it, then wait for Daddy to brace it and put it in the dining room. I remember our tree decorated at Christmas with shiny glass balls, twisted-tin icicles, and clip-on candleholders. I made chains of colorful cut paper and strings of popcorn for the finishing touches. The tiny candles glowed on Christmas Eve like the many stars above the Window that shone on the families below. The golden light from the houses spread warmth to all who lived there and to all who visited.

CHAPTER NINE

A DESERT RAINBOW

On a September day in 1937, our new governess ran into the house at Oak Creek. Miss Pope, her dyed-red hair askew, tended to talk with her hands when excited. Though petite with expressive features, she seemed large and very competent to me. On this particular day her kind, blue eyes sparkled with fear. "Mrs. Wilson, there's a big rattlesnake in front of the porch!"

Mother grabbed one of Daddy's rifles from the closet under the stairs and ran out to the yard to kill the snake. When she saw it, she exclaimed, "That's the biggest rattlesnake I ever saw in my life. It must be six feet long."

So, Mother shot it with my father's gun. When he came home, she told him about the big rattlesnake in front of the porch.

"Where is it, Bergine?" He went out and looked, then said, "Why, it's nothing but a chicken snake." When Mother looked disappointed, he glared at her. "What gun did you use?"

"Oh, I used the one under the stairs with the leather thing

that goes across — that hangs over your shoulder."

"That's my best gun, my target rifle. Did you clean it?"

"Well, Homer, I don't know how to clean a gun. Imagine a girl that grew up like I did knowing how to shoot, let alone knowing how to clean one."

Mother didn't hear the last of that for a long, long time. She vowed, "I'm not shooting any more snakes. They can be double rattlesnakes as far as I'm concerned!"

Daddy had other weapons in that closet. He chose a pistol from his service in World War I to teach Mother how to shoot for protection. She opposed this, giving reluctant agreement after telling him again that she did not want to fire any more guns.

He insisted she practice with his Luger. Mother held the pistol and pointed it at a tin can on a cedar post, then turned her head, grimaced, and fired.

My father warned, "Bergine, when I'm away from the house at night, you must shoot any intruder. Nobody in this country will come in a house without calling out first. If they do come in without warning you, they have no business there. Just shoot."

One night my father came home when Mother did not expect him. The wind blew through the trees near the east bedroom upstairs where my governess slept. Mother stayed in the bedroom across the hall. She awakened to the rustle of leaves on the willow tree and the creak of slow and quiet footsteps coming up the wooden steps. At the top of the stairway, the shuffle hesitated then started to enter the bedroom door.

Mother lunged for the pistol, ready to shoot anyone who entered the dark doorway. My father remembered in time what he had told Mother. He yelled, "Don't shoot, Bergine. It's me."

Many times my father arrived unannounced and departed suddenly when he had a crisis on the ranch. Even though he worked long hours and spent many nights away from home, he told Mother his heart stayed with us. She said to me:

There was a time when we had a real hard rain, and the water poured off Cattail Falls and ran down that dry creek past that gate from Nail's. Your daddy sheared at Double Mills at the time. I was all alone with you children here at Oak Canyon. Homer Jr. slept in the crib then.

Homer came all that way, and he walked the fence until his hands bled from the barbed wire, trying to get to us. Those creeks all came up. I was never so surprised when I looked out and there he was coming down the hill. He was so afraid that the flooding waters might reach the house or we might be harmed.

I knew those infrequent floods. Brown water roared down canyons and arroyos, carrying giant rocks with it and uprooted brush that swirled above the boulders. Floodwaters spilled wide above the banks, foaming around the tops of low bushes. The crashing sounds raised respectful fear with all of us who lived in Big Bend.

We developed skills for coping with difficult and dangerous times in this wild country. We all learned, and we all taught every day in this Texas outback. However, when the time came for my formal education, my parents chose correspondence lessons instead of driving the twenty-three miles to the closest public school at Study Butte. Those rugged roads took several hours to drive. My parents also rejected moving the family to Marathon or Alpine for the school year. Cost, convenience, and keeping the family together determined their choice.

My teacher came to us with the Nails' recommendation. She taught Julia at their ranch one year. Though Miss Pope had a Master of Arts degree, she did not find work during this part of the Depression as many schools stopped hiring women. My parents felt lucky she agreed to move to Oak Creek and help me for a year.

After breakfast each weekday, I went upstairs to our

schoolroom. I had my own old-fashioned desk of dark wood with decorative iron trim. A small groove held my pencil on the desktop. We didn't use the round hole for an inkbottle, at least I don't remember using ink for anything. I kept my tablets and colors in the little shelf. My teacher had a larger desk, a chair, and a blackboard. She also used an easel for a big tablet of paper. Except for books and Calvert materials, we used little space in that bedroom.

In 1937, families as far away as the Outback of Australia used the Calvert School courses. The Big Bend country and the Australian Outback compared nicely. Both were vast in size, sparsely populated, and the people had few modern conveniences. In fact, Calvert publications mentioned sending their materials to over fifty countries in the world. Some deliveries went by dogsled, camel caravan, or by parachute from an airplane. This curriculum fit my needs.

Each morning I saw the Window through the willow trees, their leaves rustling outside my schoolroom. Sunshine splashed a rainbow of colors on the hillsides and the birds sang constantly. This beautiful setting framed and enlarged our school space, while Miss Pope developed my mind.

It surprises me how much I remember from my Calvert work. My teacher taught me to love learning. The materials challenged me and seemed like fun rather than lessons.

We started the day with some general information. Miss Pope shared things about science, geography, and history in an informal way. "I'm training you to express yourself orally and fluently in correct English. I expect you to answer in complete sentences." Miss Pope always spoke softly and smiled.

Next, we studied new words and reviewed from my first writer booklet. We always had rules for spelling, penmanship, capitalization, and punctuation such as leaving one finger's width between words and two finger's width between sentences on wide-ruled paper. As I advanced to double-ruled paper, I left one pencil width between words and two pencil widths between sentences. Miss Pope insisted on spotless pages without rumples or finger smudges. Often, I used a cover sheet of clean paper to protect my work in progress.

In writing, we used the main words and studied them whole. In fact, in the beginning, we made complete sentences of these words then cut them for study. I did not learn alphabetically, though. After absorbing the basics, we advanced to phonics. Now I attacked sentences on my own and began to read little stories aloud. This opened a new and wonderful world.

One of the main differences between Calvert and public school writing seemed that we began with the simplest form of script, not print. Miss Pope called it vertical script and said, "It's most legible, fastest, and you can read print as similar."

Each letter ended in a curling tail that we eventually learned to join to make words. I remember myself tipping my head to the side, my tongue in the corner of my mouth, intent on getting that letter ending just right. When I did, my teacher praised my efforts, and I glowed.

She introduced letter writing as soon as I could manage enough words. Usually, these short notes went to one or both of my parents or to Julia who attended Marathon High School at this time. This way the ones I loved saw my progress and provided immediate support and praise. Oh, I liked that.

I wrote right-handed though left-handed writing was allowed for those who needed it. Some institutions at that time tried to make all young persons write with their right hands, but not the Calvert program.

After a brief break each morning for a few exercises, we did numbers. Most of this arithmetic had a practical application. I remember using counters and toy money in a play store. I used sticks to divide, breaking them into pieces to understand the whole and the parts. We worked on fractions as a new kind of division, often cutting an apple into pieces then eating the parts as a snack after our lesson. Miss

Pope said things like, "How many bunches of two are in twelve?" She taught me to tell time and measure. We made shapes like triangles by folding paper and drew circles with a piece of string tied to a nail. The spots on dominos aided in our counting.

We studied pictures, including prints of famous paintings. My favorites were the madonnas of Leonardo de Vinci, Raphael, and Michelangelo. *The Blue Boy* by Gainsborough and *The Gleaners* by Millet shine in my mind also. This beginning led to my lifetime love of painting and to my becoming an art teacher.

We had monthly tests before going on to new materials. At the end of the first grade, I wrote a fifty word story about my pet, read a story aloud, talked about what I learned, identified pictures by name and artist, memorized and recited a poem, added five numbers, subtracted two digits from three numbers using borrowing, multiplied two numbers by one, and divided with long division four numbers by one. All first graders demonstrated proficiency in these things before advancing to second grade. The individualized program did allow for personal differences though, giving needed time for mastery before testing. Luckily, with help and encouragement, I finished first and second grades in one year.

Organized school took three hours in the mornings. After lunch, we spent time studying nature and exploring our environment. We climbed hills, turned over rocks, collected leaves, and found interesting things like bleached bones. We identified plants, animals, birds, and anything that crawled or flew. Miss Pope helped me save information from magazines that related to our nature wanderings. Mother got a large pattern book from Ritchey's Store in Marathon for a scrapbook. I chose, cut, glued, drew, and wrote about our adventures in this book. During this seemingly free time, my beloved instructor asked problem-solving questions. "How is the squirrel like a rabbit? What is different about these? Why is this important? Where can this be used differently? Why do you think this?"

Outside the classroom upstairs, my governess seemed timid. Afraid of heights, she spent much time with a worried expression as we had plenty of high places in those mountains. Her fear extended to horseback riding. However, always a good sport, she rode to please me and to be a part of our excursions. I can see her going down the trail holding the saddle horn until her knuckles whitened with a determined look on her sweet face. By this time, I rode easily and had a tendency to show off for my teacher, loping on straight stretches and waving my free arm, straight hair streaming beneath my straw hat. I laughed, and she managed a weak smile, her lips pursed and eyes like a rabbit's.

* * * * *

One Saturday after February shearing in 1938 and during my second grade with Miss Pope, Daddy invited all of us to go with him on mining business. He and Harris Smith had started the Fresno Mine the year before — a quicksilver to mercury operation eleven miles north of Lajitas. On the way, my father planned to stop at the store at Terlingua, and, if time allowed, visit at Study Butte on the way back. Mother agreed, Miss Pope accepted the invitation, and I jumped up and down with excitement. The store at Terlingua had ice cream, pop, and bubble gum, all high on my list of favorites.

Daddy loaded the wooden box of dynamite for the mine and Mother packed a picnic lunch. Bluebonnets carpeted the shoulders of the dirt road as we headed west. Great patches of the royal blue blooms balanced the creams and reds of the clays near Study Butte and the beiges of Terlingua Creek. The morning sunlight hit an occasional calcite crystalline rock, causing it to sparkle and reflect bright white and sapphire blue.

By late morning we passed the crowded cemetery with its rock-covered graves crowned with white, wooden crosses, then pulled into the Company Store at Terlingua, known for its wide variety of merchandise from thread and cloth to automobiles.

Terlingua, a dusty quicksilver-mining town, had about 2,000 people, most of them Mexican. A movie house and an ice cream parlor stood next to the store. The one-room, rock jailhouse lay at the end of these buildings.

The Anglos lived in the fifteen homes west of the shop. These adobe homes had tin roofs, wooden floors, and water tanks. In addition, a wagon delivered twenty-five pounds of ice to each of these families once a week. The Mexican people lived on the east side of town in rock and adobe homes with dirt floors. They accessed free water, but hauled it themselves from the tank to their homes. Even at six, I saw these differences and thought this wasn't fair.

A friend my age, Fred Dumas, went to the Perry School, located about a block west of the store where Fred's aunt, Ruth Hale, taught. About seventy-five Mexican children and five Anglos attended the two-room facility. Fred seemed tall, quiet around girls, and interesting. The last time we visited, he talked about recess and activities like softball, kite flying, Mexican marbles, and hunting lizards. Since I studied alone, this sounded exciting. I missed playing with other children at times and imagined being included in games. Usually, the other kids at Terlingua just watched me with big, soulful eyes when I came to town. Miss Pope said they had a state certified curriculum and textbooks. I guessed that meant it was a good school.

After an ice-cream cone, we bounced on to Lajitas, then headed the eleven miles north to Fresno where Daddy visited with his partner, Harris Smith, about the new mine. They seemed concerned about materials. Mr. Smith shook his white hair, his eyes intent. My father explained how they could build using ordinary materials for these beginnings of a flotation plant. Cinnabar, heavier than surrounding dirt, sank to the bottom when mixed with water. This made it easier to separate the quicksilver-bearing ore. Since these times during the Depression made starting a new mine difficult, they tried to keep expenses low.

Finally, they smiled. Daddy left the wooden box of dynamite at the assay shed and we headed back to Study Butte — another small mercury-mining town. After we stopped at the store there, Daddy visited with Mr. Burcham, who headed this mine, while my teacher and I walked near their adobe home. The thick walls acted as insulation, making the rooms cool in summer and warm in the winter. Mrs. Burcham and her daughter, Ruby June, lived in Alpine for Ruby June's education.

Many people moved when their children needed further education, like Julia, who lived with two aunts one year in San Antonio after she had teachers at their ranch for three years. Julia told me she took her final exams over the district materials with the other students at Marathon. She and Mrs. Nail lived there during this time and will leave when Julia finishes her last two years of high school. When they return, we planned on having the Nails over to celebrate Julia's graduation and Miss Pope's departure.

My teacher pointed out the one-room school taught by Mrs. Elizabeth Bledsoe. One of her students, Bobby Eaves, called her a wonderful lady. His father, Lucian Eaves, a mining engineer at the mercury mine there, died when Bobby went to second grade. Mr. Eaves pumped company gas to a person who did not turn off his vehicle motor. The resulting explosion burned Bobby's father who died of pneumonia caused by inhaled heat. Mrs. Eaves and Bobby remained in Study Butte where she operated a boarding house.

Mrs. Bledsoe, Bobby's teacher, gave short speeches every day to the whole classroom on many subjects, hammering constantly on personal hygiene and discussing honor, ethics, and patriotism. Failure to be polite or surliness got you in big trouble fast according to Bobby, who said most of the kids were very nice, though. He felt his teacher was the least prejudiced person he ever knew, saying the young Mexican children really loved her. She rewarded them with hugs that they liked. She favored students by letting them go outside and clean erasers. Since she boarded at Bobby's home, he felt he had a favorable position. He also felt his education in a room with mixed grades and a large number of students to the teacher had great advantages. Every student in the room heard and often participated in all subject matter. Smarter kids learned advanced subjects. Slower students heard a repetition of things they didn't get too well the first time. Bobby advanced when he went to Alpine since educators there promoted him from fifth grade to seventh. This indicated to me the high quality of education at Study Butte.

By the time we returned to Oak Creek, I felt glad to continue our learning at home. Homer Jr. and I also studied our surroundings. We tried to explain many local mysteries. Although we thought and talked about unusual happenings, we never solved any of them. However, we did learn to gather information, ask questions, and guess at solutions.

One of the most unusual happenings was the strange voices heard at Oak Creek Canyon. At certain times of the day or night, we heard whispers and murmurs of people. Finally, we decided the words came from the road camp some five miles away on the dirt highway. The sounds echoing from the cliffs seemed eerie as if people talked under the oak trees when no people were around.

Many mysteries surrounded the *curanderos* — healers who used herbs and special treatments on their patients. Daddy told me many of these secret ways and potent treatments came from the Aztec heritage of the border peoples. Chata, a *curandera*, delivered many babies and treated many persons near Boquillas. I never heard of a failure by this revered lady in these treatments.

Another different happening concerned goat dogs. Down on the Rio Grande and in some other places in Chisos country, people trained dogs to care for herds of goats. A nanny adopted a young puppy placed with her, letting it nurse so it grew thinking it was a goat. As a result, the dog protected the herd from predators. People did not feed or humanize them, or they lost their willingness to live a goat's life. In my mind, I see these animals grazing on hills near Terlingua with two large dogs guarding their adopted family. This behavior fascinated me.

One mystery of the Chisos involved the old mine one mile northeast of our house at Oak Canyon. The mine looked like a crack in a bluff just north of the Window. The last time I saw it, a broken, hand-turned crank stood on a small wooden platform near the deep cave. Cool air drifted from the dark hole. A landslide covered much of the pulley mechanism. Frayed bits of rope clung to part of the winch near stone slabs that blocked the opening. My father lowered himself into the depths of this crack, but did not find anything of value. He did, however, warn us of the dangers of this old mine because of the rock formation. The stone could shift at any time, trapping or crushing anyone caught in the cavern's depths.

Stories about this old mine passed from person to person. Evelyn Burnam, who used to live here, heard some people went down and recovered some loot from an old railroad robbery. Evelyn's father, Charlie Burnam, offered to help, but these searchers flatly refused. The story goes that the robbers were later arrested with the treasure.

Julia said that a man came to visit their ranch and asked to explore the mine. Sam gave his permission. Later this person hurried from the Nail land, his wagon bed covered with a tarp and tied down with rope. Did the man recover the gold hidden there by Spaniards fleeing Indians? The mystery remains.

Waddy Burnham found a bar of silver bullion when he rode in the Chisos, but he never told where he found it. My father picked up a small, gold nugget while studying the geology of the ranch. As far as I learned, those were the only valuable finds other than natural mineral deposits such as fluoride, cinnabar, and silver.

The real treasures in Big Bend included the beautiful land

and the good people who lived and worked there. Learning and growing in this community seemed like living with a beautiful rainbow at the base of Cattail Falls. Brilliant colors reflected in the cool, refreshing pool surrounded by the lush greens of ferns. Bright memories of the many fascinating and challenging experiences color my mind with a haunting longing for that special country of mountains and desert.

Chapter Ten

CELEBRATION

We invited the Nails for a celebration at Oak Creek one glorious sunny day in June when Mrs. Nail and Julia returned after Julia's graduation from Marathon High School. Mother also wanted to do something special for Miss Pope before she left us. After a festive lunch, small gifts for my so-called sister and my teacher, and a leisurely visit on the screened porch, we left for Cattail Canyon for a swim. Sam and Daddy stayed to rest and talk.

We walked the path beyond the unused outhouse. The trail turned to go up the hill at the crumbling ruins of an old adobe wall that shielded a dump area. A bright yellow flower grew from flat, gray-green leaves near this clay soil, like a bright reminder of the past. The soft breeze, low humidity, and a higher altitude made walking comfortable. All of us dressed in long sleeves for protection from the sun. Mother and Mrs. Nail wore bonnets, the rest of us had straw hats. We looked like figures in a Millet painting marching below mountains with rust-colored bluffs. Instead of fields of wheat and grain, we went by cactus and scrub brush. The still picture gave the same feeling of happy people in a special place and time.

As we crossed the flat places between the hills, Julia and I searched the brown dirt for arrowheads, knowing that Indians had hunted in these places. I viewed the blues of the distant mountains past Burro Mesa to the west. Puffy clouds rose high in the turquoise sky like piles of new-shorn wool and cotton boles floating in the wind, a desert landscape of great beauty to me.

Descending the rocky path from the hills into Cattail Canyon, we saw ahead the dark stain of the falls on the red rock. The green oak trees seemed a carpet below us. The trail passed over the landslide of rose-colored stones crumbled from the towering cliffs of the Chisos. A lizard scurried from one slab to another then dived out of sight. As we neared the creek bottom, we heard echoes of cliff swallows calling, water trickling over gravel, and the gentle sounds of wind in the leaves of the trees. The clear liquid sometimes fell from one pool to another creating miniature falls where ferns lined the water with hints of iron deposits shimmering near shadows of stones.

We scrambled over the last large rocks. Ahead, the falls fell seventy-five feet, clear water dripping and spraying to the reservoir below as we clamored to this oasis. The depths of the pool looked blue-green, like the center of a large emerald. A natural shelf of stone jutted beneath the cascading stream, a perfect resting place for swimmers.

Julia, Homer Jr., and I took turns dressing behind several large boulders, broken free from the cinnabar cliffs ages ago. We tiptoed into the icy shallows, dreading that first gasp of cold as we sank in the crystal pool. Reflections surrounded us of red rock, gray stones, green columbine, and a few bright red flowers growing in a crevice.

The thirty-foot swim to the stone projection seemed nothing to an adult, but for me it was a special feat. I dog paddled back and forth to Julia, so proud of my new ability. We laughed and splashed, swam to the stone shelf, and floated in the clear water. My little brother waded in the shallows and turned over flat rocks for water creatures. Sunshine backlit his hair giving a halo effect. We gloried in the cold water as dragonflies and butterflies lit on the large yellow columbines. I beamed with happiness, playing with ones I loved, an idyllic time for all of us.

I remembered when Julia taught me to swim in the tank at the top of the hill from her house. The four-foot-deep water lapped around me as I clung to the metal side of the reservoir, fearful I might sink in the mossy depths. Hot sun warmed my wet hair and shoulders, but I shivered with apprehension. The harsh sounds of grasshoppers mixed with the soft lapping of water against rust-colored metal. Julia coaxed, "You can do it, Tricia." She stretched her arms towards me. I hesitated, shivered, then let go and churned my arms and legs, head thrown back and nose above water, dog paddling to my friend standing a few feet away. I felt a wonderful sense of achievement and a warm, loving presence of Julia holding me and praising my efforts. Her patience and pride did much to encourage me whenever I tried a new activity where I felt smaller or weaker than others.

* * * * *

The summer of 1938 brought much company to the ranch. Relatives and friends came to Oak Creek, and we invited our neighbors to meet them. We slept there, but often made side trips with visitors to other places on the ranch. With the help of Sam, who loaned us extra horses and saddles, we took my aunt to picnic at the head of Blue Creek. The Burnhams and Nails, plus Julia's cousins, Evelyn and Dorothy Burnam, rode with us past the tall columns of copper-colored layered rock, in strange pillars like twisted phantoms. Mother and Daddy trailed in the International with food and camping supplies.

The adults stayed at the base camp of the mountain trail

near Cedar Spring while the children climbed the side of Ward Mountain to the alum cave at the bottom of a tall bluff high above the camp. The shallow cavern, backed with a white, powder-like wall of alum, sheltered us from the June wind. From this place, I looked across the canyon to the mountains rimmed with layers of limestone, fading to a light blue in the distance. I ate some of the sour alum, which made me sick in the night. This misadventure didn't ruin our times, though.

We camped overnight before riding the winding trail that switched back and forth to the high parts of the mountains including Laguna, a meadow with waist-high grasses. As we passed a crumbling log structure, I heard the adults asking about it. We called it the Rooney cabin though Mary and John Daniels built the shelter. It amazed me to imagine them hauling their possessions by wagon to the head of Blue Creek then carrying everything they had including her good dishes up the switchbacks of these steep mountains. Here at the meadow of Laguna they hunted and grew a small amount of food. We rode on to the South Rim, a 2,000-foot precipice, where we viewed the mountains and lowlands to the Rio Grande and over seventy miles into Mexico. Clouds floated below us, and eagles rode the thermals then circled against the blue sky.

I remember Mother riding Brownie on her old cavalry saddle. She wore carpenter's overalls and held her bonnet as she looked over our ranch below, her hair parted in the middle and held back in a simple bun. My father stood near the bluff, hands on his hips above his worn chaps then pointed to a landmark in the distance. Visitors looked and talked. I stood further back from the chasm, recognizing the danger of slipping and falling. A gnarled cedar, weathered by wind and time, grew near the edge among the tall grasses and rocks. The scene gave me a feeling of awe before we remounted and began the long descent home.

Later that summer we held another picnic under the big oak trees just north of the house at Oak Canyon. After

Daddy put several watermelons under wet burlap to cool in the creek, he took Buzzy and me to Terlingua to buy blocks of ice for homemade ice cream. We carried these home, wrapped in the canvas tarp in the back of the pickup. While Mother prepared large pots of frijole beans and checked the slabs of goat meat roasting in the oven, Daddy turned the ice-cream freezer and packed it with salt. Friends and neighbors from as far away as Fresno (north of Lajitas) parked in the shade of the trees near the long shop table used for holding food that day. Many brought covered dishes of salads and fresh-baked desserts to put with Mother's peach cobblers sitting under clean dishtowels on this table.

I entertained the children with my new game of elevator, using a fifty-foot length of rope we threw halfway over a horizontal limb of the big, leaning oak. After we tied one end of the rope to the middle of a two-foot long stick, we had an elevator. We took turns sitting on the stick with the rope between our legs, then reached to the other end of the line and kept pulling until we lifted ourselves to the overhead limb. We had great fun!

My little brother and another boy played with little metal cars in the dirt bank by the creek. They built roads and bridges for their tiny vehicles. I heard them buzz and talk as they played.

After we finished the desserts with ice cream and cold watermelon, the ladies carried the leftovers to the house and the men stood around or came to the screened-in porch to visit.

Julia and several Burnhams walked with some of the children up Oak Creek, where we explored and waded in the stream. On the way back, some of us picked fresh peaches for friends to carry home. The peach fuzz tickled my arms and a faint scent of sap from the trees wafted in the air. The echoes of children laughing filled my memories of that happy day.

Other memories of joyous times remained. Ada and Elmo Johnson had a yearly fish fry at their home on the river southeast of Castolon. Several of the men caught large catfish for this occasion and cooked them over a pit. Other people went down to the Rio Grande to swim, but my father wouldn't let us get in the water. He said the river was dangerous with treacherous whirlpools and undertows. Mother helped the ladies set the long tables under some trees with the many foods. Tall cane and willows rustled by the river where the water shimmered in the sunlight. Several turtles sunned on some rocks by a salt cedar tree. The sounds of cicadas and murmurs of people laughing and talking surrounded us that festive day.

Across the Rio Grande in the distance, I saw the buildings of the little town of Santa Helena in front of the blue cliffs of the Mesa de Anguila. A few cottonwoods grew near the water closer to Johnson's, their yellow-green leaves light against the darker bluffs.

Elinor Cartledge told me she helped Mrs. Johnson make potato salad for the big meal. The Mexican workers attended the barbeque. According to Elinor, the help dug a deep pit where whole kid goats and large parts of beef seasoned and wrapped in burlap baked and sizzled, buried in the pits full of hot chunks of mesquite roots. An open fire kept a washtub of frijoles cooking. Spicy smells of roasting meat and bubbling coffee mixed with the sights of the long table crowded with bowls of food and the bright red slices of watermelon. Groups of people laughed, glad to be together again.

Mrs. Johnson, slender and attractive, wore a pretty cotton dress with a skirt that flowed in the breeze. On her head she had a wide-brimmed straw hat with little, red pom-poms hanging from the brim. She loved children and always smiled at me. Mr. Johnson, an average-sized, thinner man was known for his fair treatment of the Mexican people who crossed the river to trade at their shop.

A large adobe building housed their store and home. The porch had a high ceiling, perhaps twelve feet tall with pine logs supporting river cane. Mounted deer horns lined the adobe walls. Below these racks hung groupings of large photographs of the area, done by their friend, W. D. Smithers. Under the pictures, chairs and benches of twig furniture lined the wall by the tall, crank victrola. As I looked through to the store, I saw dozens of pelts lining the wall, traded or sold by local Mexicans from both sides of the Rio Grande. Their store catered to the people living in lower Big Bend and to Mexicans who crossed the river to sell their big bundles of wood, chino grass, and furs. After selling their wares, these natives returned to Mexico with staple foods and such things as cloth for sewing.

I remember the generosity of Elmo and Ada. Our mailbox held oversize packages in the outsized container. In season, the Johnsons left one or two melons in our box when they drove to Marathon.

Ada and Elmo Johnson not only welcomed neighbors and friends for their annual picnic, but also had parties for the children of the area. These local Mexican children looked forward to special treats and gifts from the Johnsons at Christmas time.

The Johnsons raised some goats on their pastureland where they grew cotton for a time, but now raised mostly vegetables and feed under irrigation.

As we drove home from the Johnson picnic, we passed Castolon, the site of an old cavalry station from the times of Pancho Villa. The Wayne Cartledge family had a store there and farmed cotton on the river land. Their ranch bordered ours. The lengthening shadows from the tall blue escarpment of Santa Elena Canyon darkened the valley floor. The slash where the Rio Grande cut through stone forming the opening loomed on our left, its 1500-foot cliffs towering above the river. Several burros browsed near the water, turning to watch as we passed.

Julia told me this place where the river pours out of Santa Elena Canyon was where her father loved to fish. Her family and the Waddy Burnham family went there every summer and camped out, spending one or two nights there. She remembered the sand being blazing hot on her bare feet.

Sam, a strong swimmer, would swim across the treacherous Rio Grande to set up a trotline. Fresh fish added change to their diet too. Fishing sounded special to me, but we never seemed to find time for this.

Later, as we continued home from Johnson's, I saw a cocky roadrunner racing along the dirt road — his red-rimmed eyes glared at me as if to say he dared us to pass. These ground birds leave tracks like an X. When I looked at the print, I couldn't tell which way the bird ran.

We reached Oak Creek as the sun glowed orange on the Window. Later, my father set off a few firecrackers. He had a tradition of fireworks and watermelon on Independence Day. Bright colors burst in the air and we waved sparklers, watching the sizzle with showers of white light, a beautiful end to a glorious day.

* * * * *

Once in a while, other area ranchers had barbeques including a dance that lasted all night with children sleeping on pallets on the floor while the adults talked and told stories. This gave the children a chance to see other kids, something they didn't do often in such isolated country. It also provided the adults a relaxing, fun-filled time for visiting and seeing distant friends.

When we went to Terlingua, we saw the movie house and the ice cream parlor. Fred Dumas remembered the Mexican people having dances once a month on a large cement square, three blocks east of the Company Store. These special occasions featured music with guitar and accordion. Later, local men poured a cement slab for skating by both the children and adults.

Fred told me more about his fun at Terlingua. They didn't play "Forts," but used the prospector holes scattered around the town. These holes, some six to ten feet deep, made great hideouts when they covered the tops with sotol poles and a final layer of greasewood.

All the boys carried pocket knives at Terlingua. In fact, boys carried knives through high school at Alpine. I remember carrying a folding knife when at the ranch, but didn't when I went to school in Alpine where the girls played jacks and jumped rope.

Fred and the other boys carried slingshots made by using a Y-shaped mesquite limb or a forked deer horn for the frame. Two strands of rubber inner tube and the tongue made from an old shoe created the sling. Fred told me, "It made a formidable weapon. You could shoot a small rock fifty yards with good accuracy. We set up old bottles to aim at."

Boys at Terlingua played Mexican marbles, a gambling type game, during all of the year. Instead of shooting on the ground at your enemy, the player stood then dropped his marbles into a cup-sized hole in the ground. If an even number of marbles ended in the hole, the shooter kept all the marbles. If an odd number ended in the hole, the other player won. They found this winner-take-all activity great fun.

Other boys activities included spinning tops to try to knock a chunk out of your opponent's wooden top and making and flying kites of strips of wood from old egg crates and covering the frames with brown wrapping paper. They made the tails of rags and got the string from the Company Store.

For entertainment, the local men poured a cement slab near the Perry School. The children and adults used this for skating. Fred later told me, "You and your family were over at Terlingua and parked by the skating rink. All of the Anglo kids were amazed at you because of your blonde hair! We had never seen a girl with anything but dark hair. Anyway, you were the center of attention for a while."

Also for local fun, some residents at Study Butte dammed the creek that ran by Burcham's house to make a swimming hole. Ruby June Burcham (Wilhelm) said her brothers taught her to swim there. In the summer with the long evenings after supper, her family sometimes drove to Terlingua creek and found a place to swim.

Another friend, Bobby Eaves from Study Butte, remembered his mother allowing him much independence when he lived there. He had two donkeys and loved to ride them everywhere. Mrs. Eaves let him and one of his Mexican friends ride the burros to Santa Elena Canyon where they camped for several days by themselves and fished.

I envied Bobby and Fred having friends their age where they lived. Most of the time, the only person I had for play was my little brother. Mother did let us go and do what we wanted to as she figured we knew what we were doing. She liked to read and do handwork while we climbed all over the mountains and hills of the Chisos when we didn't ride our horses or go exploring. The quest was the thing. Here we learned to appreciate not only the wild landscape with its twisted rock formations and deep canyons where the call of a wren echoed with the screech of the hawk, but also the softer, gentler sight of a baby fawn tottering in tall grass. Hiking and exploring this unusual land seemed a constant adventure. We gloried in the feather from a white-winged dove, treasured a rock that sparkled, collected a twisted length of bleached mesquite, or found an unusual cactus in bloom.

When we climbed in the mountains and hills, we did not think much about risks. We knew the dangers. Much of the time we went barefoot on the rough ground with no thought of peril. After a period of time, the bottoms of our feet grew thick calluses.

Our solitary life changed when Buzzy and I went to headquarters where we played with Frances Felts, the foreman's daughter. Early one morning, Frances and I went out to the round pen to watch her father whip train some horses. Tall poles formed the circular enclosure to keep out distractions from the skittish colt. A nubbing post marked the center of the circle. Lott put a young, unbroken gelding in the pen. When Mr. Felts cracked his long whip, the horse ran in a circle near the poles until it came back to Lott. The colt danced and turned, throwing its head high. The golden mane waved and flowed. A slight odor of dry manure mingled with horse sweat floated toward Frances and me, hiding and watching on the other side of the plank gate. After many repetitions of the pop of the lash and the running to Lott, the horse began to come to the sound of the crack of braided leather. Eventually, the horse ran to Mr. Felts whenever he popped his whip.

We hurried through lunch that day before running outside to build our fort. After picking a perfect place, we each carried flat rocks, stacked these into walls leaving openings for a door and a window. We thatched the roof with greasewood over sotol and lechuguilla poles. This thatch smelled vaguely of wax. Our last efforts focused on protection for our stockade, gathering and laying prickly pear cactus leaves in the little path leading to the fort. Now a barefoot person couldn't approach our fortress. Soon, we abandoned the site and began another, more elaborate fortress. The building was the important thing.

We found climbing and exploring important also. Frances and I didn't think much about danger. Both of us knew what might be harmful and knew where to watch for snakes. Signal Peak, my favorite scaling place, loomed beyond the stock pens.

Leaving early on a cool morning, we walked over the first rim of rock to the top of that flat mesa. Fuzzy, brilliant red velvet ants darted around the volcanic rocks. An occasional giant tarantula crept beneath the ocotillo and sotol. Its black, hairy legs and body emphasized the caramel-colored head. Though it looked fearsome, we knew it as harmless. It leaped, causing us both to scurry backwards. The wasp that hunted it, if successful, paralyzed the big spider then dragged it to her nest in the ground where she laid her eggs. Later the babies fed on the comatose tarantula. Life had its stark times in the desert.

As we continued our climb, the morning sun threw warm

light on the opposite cliffs of Ward Mountain. We trudged toward the second rim of red rock some forty feet high to a tall, shallow cave. We scrambled at a sixty-degree angle to the stone recesses where we rested. The cavern opening framed the valley below, like a window to the floor of Blue Creek. Headquarters looked like a cluster of dollhouses with the people as busy as insects. From this vantage point we viewed the beiges and greens of the gullies and hills to Santa Elena Canyon, a dark shadow in the blue mesas in the distance.

After a short rest, we clamored out of the cave, turned right along the bluff to a crack in the rocks. Here we climbed up this break, grabbing the stems of a few bushes and toeing onto cracks and shelves then trudged to the top rim. The angle of the mountain as we approached the top circle of stone seemed much steeper than it looked from the house. We inched our way up the twenty-foot rim filled with cracks and fissures. We did not realize the danger of the loose deposits until we clung some ten feet up the twenty-foot edge. As the rocks crumbled and fell, they bounced and rolled threatening to send us head first down the steep mountainside. The wind whipped against my back, and I felt I might never make it to the top of the peak. If I fell, the tumble and roll over gravel, rock slabs, cactus, and brush might be a thousand feet. I crept to the flat, circular summit of Signal Peak testing each handhold and every foothold until crawling to the top. Frances and I grinned and turned, enjoying our success. The panorama of the Chisos Mountains lay to our north, Mule Ear Peaks to our south, Burro Mesa to our west, and the giant, rust-colored boulders by the back path below us. From this high point we stood at the center and viewed most of the Wilson ranch.

As children growing up in Big Bend, we used ingenuity and imagination to keep ourselves entertained. We had few store-bought toys, so most of our activities used materials found at home or in nature. Memories of the good times in Big Bend seemed like a collage of dreams.

PART II

TROUBLED TIMES

I will lift up mine eyes unto the hills,

from whence cometh my help.

My help cometh even from the Lord,

which made heaven and earth.

He will not suffer thy foot to be moved;

he that keepeth thee will not slumber.

Psalm 121:1–3

Chapter Eleven

DUST CLOUDS THE HORIZON

To fashion a better life, the people of Big Bend worked long hours, adapted to the desert climate, and did without most amenities. The coming of the Great Depression and the associated crippling drought tested all of us who lived there. Life, difficult enough in this rough country, became further strained by failing banks and falling prices for beef, wool, and mohair. A deadly brew of little or no money coupled with decreased forage for ranch stock stressed ranchers to the breaking point like limbs blown low in a storm.

The Depression, starting with the stock market crash of October 1929, brought disaster to many banks and financial institutions. Businesses collapsed across the country, followed by high unemployment. Initially people failed to recognize what happened. My father wrote his thoughts about bad times to Mother on July 12, 1930:

> I am going from the ranch to Juno this afternoon to look at some sheep and goats. Don't expect busi-

ness to make any rapid change for the better before spring as it is going to be a slow process. It looks like everything the producer will have to sell this fall will probably be sold at a loss. It will be a gradual recovery and probably not felt very much until next spring. I didn't intend to criticize your business ability. This depression has lasted longer and dropped further than most people expected. You should hold on to your stock as conditions will no doubt be more rosy next spring.

1930 brought optimism to my father about the economy and a feeling that his money problems should cease by 1931. He did not see the magnitude of the financial crisis, nor did he realize the slow, agonizing recovery ahead. Others lacked this insight as well.

In some ways, those who lived in the Chisos and surrounding foothills fared better than those in towns and cities. Ranchers raised their own meat and hunted wild animals for food. They grew gardens and crops and believed in helping each other with work projects. Except for staple foods such as sugar, salt, flour, frijoles, and salt pork, they grew everything on their land. Sam Nail even grew frijoles west of his ranch house below Burro Mesa.

People out of work looked for non-existent jobs. Many town dwellers did not have enough money to buy needed food and other necessities. The ideal of self-sufficiency, highly valued at this time, caused families to suffer physically and emotionally.

Both town dwellers and ranchers did without new clothing and other desired items in order to meet obligations so they wouldn't lose their homes and land. Most of those in the lower Big Bend managed to keep their holdings although one rancher on the south side of the Chisos Mountains lost eight sections that bordered our land when the Del Rio Wool and Mohair Company foreclosed on him. This institution took over that ranch then sold it to Boye

Babb in 1934 with the goats and wild horses that remained on the ranch.

My father had 116 loans on land throughout the Depression. In 1933, these loans to individuals and to the state had interest rates from three to eight percent. By 1934, he consolidated his loans with the Federal Land Bank of Houston, Texas, at a rate of three percent, cutting his interest costs to less than half. This helped his finances considerably, though these payments appeared only on paper. Mother said, "They gave us ninety dollars a month to live on for everything. The rest went to the bank."

The mining engineering operations began with the Fresno Mine venture in Big Bend with Harris Smith as my father's partner at the new quicksilver mine. In 1936, Daddy borrowed more money, this time from relatives, to finance mining exploration and development. These loans, held by his brother, a sister, and his mother, all of Del Rio, Texas, had an interest rate of eight percent. Mother said she and Daddy believed in keeping business separate from family matters. However, if she and my father must borrow from family, they met their obligations the same as at the bank. Lending or borrowing from relatives carried risks. She felt borrowing money lost friends and at times alienated relatives if not repaid.

Terrible dust storms hit Marathon and northern Big Bend in the spring of 1930. Mother said dark clouds of debris blew so thick that people in Marathon could not see to walk or drive. Dirt sifted through cracks around doors and windows causing a thin layer of dust to settle inside homes and buildings. These storms continued intermittently through 1934 when most land in Big Bend received some rain. We were lucky in the Chisos as the mountains and foothills drew more rainfall than the surrounding lowlands.

The long drought and dust storms paralyzed many ranching operations. Without food and water, much of their livestock, as well as wildlife, died. Government inspectors from the loan companies were sent out to check livestock.

They came to our ranch yearly, expecting an account of all the sheep, goats, horses, mules, and cattle that we had. Since we only raised sheep and goats, the cattle difficulties that others had did not affect us. As more and more cattle weakened and died, the government built a program to help those in drought-stricken areas who raised stock. They paid a low price for the dying cattle and then destroyed them.

I asked neighbors about these problems and other difficulties during the 1930s. Evelyn Burnam (Fulcher) told me of her family's experiences during the Depression:

> I was in Nurses' Training at Hotel Dieu in El Paso at the time when we had such a terrible drought in addition to the Depression. I got two weeks leave every year to go home and was there at the time when the cattle couldn't survive any longer in Big Bend. Ranchers down here did not have access to feed (hay and cattle cubes) as they do now. They chopped the leaves off the sotol heads and fed the heads to the cattle until the sotol was all gone. The cattle were nothing but skin and bones. At that time the government had employees to come down and shoot the cattle. They were not allowed to use any meat from them, but it made little difference as they had no meat on them. As I remember they paid the ranchers from $4.00 to $6.00 a head for the cattle they shot.

When I asked Julia about the Depression in Big Bend, she told me the Nails' story:

> I vividly remember the dust storms and trust me, you have never seen anything like the ones we had during the Depression. They were so bad you could see just a few feet in front of you. This was during the drought I spoke of when the cattle died. I can remember walking home from school in

Marathon and barely being able to see and breathe. I don't know whether those awful dust storms reached the ranch. If I heard, I don't remember. I do know that the ones we had later were nothing to compare with those early ones.

Julia felt this terrible drought coinciding with the Depression finally "brought the ranchers to their knees." She thought this made it easy for the state government to come in and take the land for a national park. When many of the cattle died and they couldn't afford feed for the others, the Nails cut sotol. During that terrible drought, even sotol did not save the cattle. The federal government's program to shoot the weakest cattle at least saved the Nails from taking a total loss.

The Nails got Miss Pope as a teacher because she could not find a job even though she had her Master of Arts Degree. It became cheaper for them to hire a governess than to rent a house in town. Some of the ranchers such as the Burnhams and Todds already had houses in Marathon. The Burnhams built their house in about 1928 when cattle prices had improved. Julia felt times became better then as her father put in many improvements on the ranch such as pipelines and water tanks. When the stock market crashed, few could get money.

Julia told me workers who came by their place agreed to work in return for room and board, a common practice in the depths of the Depression.

The Nails seldom spoke of their worries in front of Julia, and most parents seemed to shield their children from the financial realities. In her eyes, Julia's family fared well compared to so many people who lived in the cities. They always had a garden and could kill a calf in the winter when the weather became cold enough to keep meat. They shared what they had and Julia said, "Your father always brought us meat when he killed a kid, Tricia."

After the bank closed in Marathon, some merchants did

not extend credit. This created another difficulty for many people. The stores did extend the Nails credit so they could get flour, sugar, coffee and beans plus tobacco, so essential to Julia's father. When they sold the calves in the fall, they paid their bills and started running up another grocery bill. She credits this experience with her learning not to buy something if she could not pay for it, another lesson taught during the Depression.

Other lessons proved difficult. Many felt women took jobs away from men who needed the employment to support their families. Married women found this a particular truth. Ruth Todd (McIver) told me about hiring women as teachers. "I taught school for a few years at Marathon when I first began teaching...Unfortunately, they didn't hire women after the hard times hit in the 1930s." Ruth held strong feelings about the results of these hard times. "You just knew that you could count on each other then...and now. Most of the time we don't need each other. I think young people feel they're not needed, don't have to work, and don't have a commitment to the community."

The Wilson ranch wasn't like the schools. Most of the workers on the Wilson ranch proved to be men, but wives and grown daughters did appear on the labor records during the Depression. Some of these worked as cooks or bookkeepers, but I am sure Lunetta Felts received the same pay for ranch work as any of the men.

Economic conditions on our ranch deteriorated as the times worsened. At first my father's excitement grew. In a letter to my mother in 1930, he wrote:

> I hardly know where to start as so much has happened and so much remains to be done. The financial depression plus the drought has placed the stock business in a very dangerous position for the present. Sheep are practically being given away at the present time for lack of feed on account of financial pressure. I have never seen anything like

it since I have been in the business.

Now is the opportune time to go in the sheep business, so Earl, George, and I are trying to locate another ranch. Land has depreciated quite a bit, too...All you have to do to buy sheep now is to have the range and exchange paper at the bank. Lambs can be bought for one half of what they're worth. It is actually the best chance I've had to make money in the sheep business, and I hope we can put off our wedding a few weeks until we can make the proper trade and buy all the sheep we can handle.

Love, Homer.

They did marry as planned. He did not buy another ranch, but did purchase more livestock for his place in the Chisos. However, Daddy's optimistic attitude changed as wool and mohair prices plummeted and prices for sheep and goats plunged. As the Depression dragged on and money became tighter, he began to have real financial difficulties. He made payments on his many loans and also needed to meet the payroll for his workers. By 1934, wool and mohair prices began to go up, but not enough to solve his difficulties. At the end of 1935 and the beginning of 1936, he did not have enough cash to pay his men. He promised to pay them as soon as he could if they stayed with him. Only one man left because of this. Later, this foreman returned and asked for his old job back. However, my father told him he could not rehire him as the man deserted Daddy when he needed him.

The number of hired hands reflected our financial situation. In 1932 and 1933, fifteen laborers worked on the Wilson ranch. In 1934, this number dropped to fourteen and by 1935 only seven men worked on our place. 1936 showed the number of workers up to fourteen again and in 1937 the number of laborers grew to nineteen. This upward trend in our ranch employment continued until the number topped at twenty-three in 1941, the official end of the Depression.

As far as I know, we did not have the terrible dust storms with this drought in the Chisos. Good forage in the foothills of the mountains with plenty of water for the sheep and goats kept down losses from the drought. We did cut some sotol for feed at that time, but not in great quantities. The fact that my father had a policy of not overstocking his land, plus his plan for alternating pasture use, contributed to our economic survival.

In 1936, my father and Harris filed their first mining claims to begin the Fresno Mine north of Lajitas. This mercury mine began production in 1937, but put an added financial strain on my father.

In 1937, he changed his Federal Land Bank loans to the Producers Wool & Mohair Company of Del Rio, Texas. He shipped his wool and mohair sacks to this house where they credited his account. Both the Federal Land Bank and Producers Wool & Mohair Company required detailed accountings of all expenses. This included the names of ranch workers and such small expense items as a sack of Bull Durham tobacco for a ranch hand.

The low point of the rough years for the Wilson ranch occurred in that crucial time of 1935 going into 1936. During those months of no money, we did without and persevered. We saved and reused containers as did our neighbors. I called us conservationists. We believed in recycling anything reusable. Mother washed the bright-patterned materials from sugar sacks and made tea towels, quilt pieces, and dresses. Even as a child, I found it exciting when a friend in Midland sent me a box of hand-me-down clothing.

Mother's green bowl symbolized the Depression for me. On one of our trips to Fresno, we stopped at the Study Butte store. Mother stared at a simple, glazed, ceramic mixing bowl on a high shelf. "Look, Homer. Isn't that bowl beautiful?" She smiled, and her large brown eyes widened.

"Go ahead and get it if you wish, Bergine." He seemed to know how much she wanted it. His voice lowered, and his blue eyes twinkled.

"But, we don't have enough money, Homer."

I thought of all the things she didn't buy and her sharing what she had. I wanted her to have the bowl also.

"If you want it, get it," he snapped.

Daddy did buy the green bowl and Mother cherished it until she died in 1991.

During the leanest years of the Depression, we turned to barter on occasion, trading a goat or some homegrown peaches for other supplies at the Study Butte store. Mother fretted about this practice as the loan company required an accounting of all livestock.

"Homer, we could lose the ranch by trading a goat!"

He glared, irritation showing at the corners of his mouth. "What in the ____ do you think they would do with the land if they got it?"

Others agonized as well. Many Mexican citizens passed through the ranch during these lean years. The massive drought extended into northern Mexico where the people suffered from unemployment and meager wages even when they found employment. Living in poverty, as did great numbers in our country, many drifted across the Rio Grande into the Big Bend. Frequently they begged for the heart of the maguey or the centers of sotol plants. These they roasted for food. They also requested the blossoms of the giant daggers and beans from mesquite trees.

The Window framed difficult times for all living creatures in the hills and across the plains below. If the economy didn't affect lives, the stark and bitter drought wrought trouble for the people and other living things.

Chapter Twelve

ADDED PANORAMA

To address the problems of no money, high unemployment, and the desperate feelings of helplessness and hopelessness, government programs began giving employment to people across the country. One of these programs, the Civilian Conservation Corps, started in Big Bend in 1934. Headquartered in the Basin above the Window of the Chisos Mountains, the CCC camp gave needed work and provided projects such as building retaining walls and bridges that improved road service. We, with our neighbors, considered these young men and their supervisors our friends.

Once during the time of this CCC camp, Mother and Daddy took fresh peaches to a friend in the Basin who wished to make brandy. The man, an employee at the camp, had a wife opposed to alcohol of any kind. Several days before, he and Mother peeled the fruit and left it in a large crock to ferment. They checked their concoction a few days later, then stood planning their project. Without warning, the wife of the CCC employee started down the hill. She seemed curious about her husband and his friends. Mother stood near the fermenting brew as the lady approached. Mother whispered, "Don't worry, Fritz. I'll just sit on the crock."

She hurried to spread her skirts, hiding the bubbling container. She perched there and visited as the wife approached. Now and then strange, gurgling noises came from under Mother's clothing. Who knows what the manager's wife thought as she heard the bubbling sounds. Fortunately, being polite, the lady didn't mention the rumbling if she heard it.

My parents and our neighbors didn't realize the coming of the small state park and the CCC camp signaled a move toward a future national park and the loss of their lands. In 1934, they welcomed the boys camped in the Basin.

One of the young men from this CCC camp liked to climb through the Window and visit with us at Oak Creek. James Owens had a friendly smile and eager demeanor. He loved to walk and explore the Chisos Mountains. He also enjoyed visiting, and we liked hearing about the new camp and his adventures. James lounged on the screened porch and told us, "I was assigned to do clerical work for R.D. Morgan, project superintendent. I arrived in the Chisos Mountains by truck from Lampasas with the enrollee records. It was about 10:00P.M. when we came over Panther Pass in full moonlight and drove into the Chisos Basin. I had never been on a mountain higher than 500 feet, so this was a very scary experience for me."

At first, James slept in a tent, but soon moved into a newly built wooden building. He explored Big Bend when he finished his clerical duties and camp activities such as washing clothes, playing basketball or participating in boxing matches. Since the Wilson ranch bordered the Basin on the west with Oak Canyon and on the south with Emory Peak, Laguna, Boot Springs, and the South Rim, we had frequent visits with James.

Once he climbed down from the Basin by way of the

Window, then hiked from our house the seven miles past the ridges of volcanic rock, the shearing pens below Ward Springs, up the hills and down to Blue Creek. From there he paced up the canyon between tall mountains, their blue cliffs and red rocks towering above him. He scrambled up the winding trail from Cedar Springs to Laguna.

At the southern end of Laguna, James lay down to rest under an oak tree. He enjoyed a peaceful time with the cool, mountain breezes blowing gently and the birds singing in the trees. Something made him feel a presence watching him. He looked around to an outcropping of boulders where a panther stared down from the rocky perch. Its tawny coat blended with the stones, but silhouetted the animal against the darker oak leaves. James remembered my father's advice to not show fear, and made himself appear as large and aggressive as possible. He jumped to his feet, yelled, and waved his arms, and the cougar ran into Blue Creek Canyon. By the time James returned to his home camp, he had walked a total of twenty-seven miles in one day.

Mr. Owens continued exploring on the Wilson ranch. Once he climbed down the towering, red cliffs above Cattail Falls where he swam in the reservoir above the waterfall. He floated and splashed away the summer heat. The cold water cascaded past the enclosed grotto to the crystal pool below. He told us he loved the wild beauty of Big Bend.

Others from the CCC camp had less luck. A young recruit found himself lost near Mule Ear Peaks for several days before a search party found him. Another man fell from the spillway called the "Pour Off" at the Window to the jagged rocks over seventy feet below. It took three days to find him in this rugged place. He went on an adventure alone, a practice my father viewed as very dangerous. If anything bad happened, who might go for help?

James enjoyed searching the mountains and hillsides as well as exploring other parts of Big Bend including the canyons of the Rio Grande. He admired many of the people he met on these forays. He talked of my father as his friend and mentor, who even gave him a panther skin once, though James could not have the skin tanned and had to bury it later.

When Mr. Owens returned to Big Bend some twenty-five years later after the area became a national park, he spent much time photographing the mountains and desert of his CCC years. Saddened by many of the changes, he missed the vanished homes of early settlers, removed by Park authorities. He found much of the wildlife gone and remembered the herds of fifteen to thirty deer trailing the mountains in the years between 1934 and 1936. He found parts of Big Bend crowded with visitors, but said that Nature would prevail over civilization.

Another CCC camper told of his experiences when he spoke at a fifty-year reunion of the Big Bend National Park in 1995. He talked about his years as a truck driver and mechanic in the Basin of the Chisos Mountains. He qualified for the camp by having been on relief, being between the ages of eighteen and twenty-five, and by being male. His Dad moved his birthday from September to July so he could meet the age requirement.

Mr. Bowers said he arrived by train at Marathon at two o'clock in the morning. A cold rain fell. After piling into a 1934 Chevrolet truck, he and the other recruits began their trip from Marathon to the CCC camp in the Basin. As they crossed the washouts at the bottom of the mountains, they held onto the bows of the truck to avoid sliding. Shortly after passing Tornillo Creek, they began to ascend.

Mr. Bowers remembered:

> We began a steady climb. This was up the lower end of Green Gulch. Had we not been numb we would have noted increased cold. The road wound in and out and across the creek bed and then up grades of twenty and thirty percent, then down similar grades. Finally, we arrived and were

deposited in a tent that had been a mess hall. It was pitch dark and we had no idea where we were. I have never been colder before or since.

As daylight came, we saw great splendor and utter devastation. We were completely surrounded by mountains of solid rock and rock slides. There had been a great rainstorm prior to our arriving and there was water running off the mountains everywhere. There were waterfalls, cataracts, streams, and rivulets all over. The devastation was fifty or more tents flat on the ground. Only one was standing and soon we saw a slicker-clad figure come out and loosen the tie-down ropes.

He recounted many tales about the CCC experiences. One story, told originally by Julia Nail about her father, Sam Nail, at the second Pioneer Reunion in Big Bend, came from Mr. Bowers:

I was returning to camp one day from Marathon in the summer of 1935, possibly 1936, when I came upon a black touring car with no top (not with the top lowered) stopped in the middle of the road. This was some six or seven miles north of Maravillas Creek. The hood on the right side was raised and an older gentleman was peering down at the engine. I don't believe he introduced himself to me or paid any particular attention to who I might be. His first words were something to the effect, "He just quit on me." He did not appear to be either perturbed or aggravated that "He had quit." At first glance I observed that the ignition distributor was held in place by two or three pieces of wire. The body of the distributor that extended into the engine block was broken just above where it was secured to the block. No doubt the distributor body had rotated enough due to vibration-loosened wires to disturb ignition timing and stop the engine. He said, "I believe if we put a wire from here to here he will go." We borrowed a piece of wire from the nearest pasture fence and installed it as he directed. The engine started without hesitation. I lowered and fastened the hood, and he drove off with a big grin and a wave of thanks. I never saw him again that day or later.

William Bowers told his daughter, "My experience at the CCC camp in Big Bend is where I started my manhood."

During these hard times of the Depression, the locals and the "boys" helped each other when possible and learned from each other.

At this time, the vista from the Window went both ways. The brick-red cliffs viewed the hills and mesas of the desert below, and also guarded the mountain basin above like an hourglass of time draining down on hurting people and parched lands.

Chapter Thirteen

FOG CURTAINS THE WINDOW

Mother appreciated the arts and enjoyed those who painted and did photography — neither common vocations in our practical country. Fred Darge, a German artist, spent his vacations from his job as a night watchman in Dallas painting pictures in Big Bend.

Known for his beautiful landscapes, he captured the unusual reds and browns of the Chisos Mountains as well as the blues and dull greens of the lowlands. When Fred came to paint, he stayed with us at Oak Creek, with the Nails below Burro Mesa, or with the Burnhams below Green Gulch. Once, when the Burnhams left their house for a time, Mr. Darge stayed at their home to paint. While Fred bunked there, Mother's sister and a friend from St. Louis stopped at the ranch house to ask directions to our place. The late afternoon sun cast long shadows from the mesquite and sotol on the hillsides. My aunt bounced up to the porch and asked, "Where is your bathroom?"

"Oh, anywhere out there," said Darge as he waved his arm in a careless manner toward the hillside of cactus and grasses.

Mother called Fred a character and an eccentric. I saw him as a quiet man who didn't talk about himself, who was average sized, and something of a loner. He never mentioned his past or a family — if he had one — and spoke in an abrupt, gruff manner when I asked him questions. I loved to sit on a rock and watch him paint the Window. He saw and captured the glory of the mountains and towering cloudbanks. He painted in early-morning light or the late afternoon sun, dabbing and brushing the rich siennas, umbers, and cerulean blues as he captured the magic scenery like jewels on display.

W. D. Smithers, a photographer, also came to Big Bend on vacations in the 1930s and early 1940s from San Antonio and stayed with Elmo and Ada Johnson at their farm about fifteen miles southeast of Castolon. He said he built an underground dark room at Johnson's farm where he developed his film and printed his photographs. He made the camera he used to take pictures of Oak Canyon, the South Rim, and Boot Canyon.

Smithers spent time in different parts of the region. His photographs during World War I and the times of Pancho Villa showed the life of the Cavalry in Big Bend, some mining activities, and the hauling of goods over early-day roads. The pictures he took in the 1930s and 1940s focused on the life of the people of the region and the beauty of the unusual landscapes. He recorded scenes of Oak Creek, the Sam Nail home, and ranch scenes in the high parts of the Chisos. Not only did Mr. Smithers share the photos with us, he also told us stories about his experiences while staying on the Rio Grande. We learned the latest tales about *curanderos* (healers), goat dogs (dogs raised with goats), eagles killing young antelope, and the progress on the airstrip at Johnson's farm. Mr. Smithers looked smart and handsome wearing a leather jacket, white scarf blowing in the wind, and a leather flight cap with straps dangling and goggles atop his head.

We, as well as the Nails, had frequent company. Friends came to stay, relatives visited, and many strangers arrived unannounced. Politicians wanted to look at the land as plans for a state park and a possible national park crystallized. Scientists and professors researched plants, animals, fossils, and geology. All of these people stayed with those who lived here. Since the Burnhams, Nails, and our place had access to the high, mountainous parts of the Chisos, most of them stayed at one of these places. As some of these visitors wished to take side trips into the mountains, this required riding equipment and horses that the ranchers provided free of charge as a courtesy. We gave places to stay and backcountry transportation when needed. Not only this, but these daylong trips took time away from regular ranch work. However, locals showed their usual warm hospitality.

My parents didn't complain to visitors, but they did talk about the visitor problem. Mother, who was not raised with the Code of the West, took issue with the many strangers staying at Oak Creek. Once, during shearing, our busiest time, some people came on horseback, borrowed horseshoes for all their horses, and stayed five days. Blue Creek didn't have enough beds for the man's wife and daughter, so my father had to make the trip night and morning over seven miles of bad road to bring her and the girl to our house to stay.

Mother also felt irritated when many of these strangers forgot to say "Thank you."

Of all the people who came to view the proposed parkland, the only visitor who thanked Mrs. Nail for her hospitality was Roger Toll, Superintendent of Yellowstone National Park at the time. He gave her a little book about Yellowstone. Sam always shared extra horses and saddles for the trips up Blue Creek to see the high slopes of the Chisos where riders walked under the one hundred foot pines at Boot Canyon, viewed the panorama of Mexico in the distance from the South Rim, and enjoyed the red-layered rock formations as they wound down the steep trail to headquarters.

We had company from the Texas Legislature and also from Congress. Researchers seemed fascinated by the unusual land, growing plants, and living creatures of Big Bend. Mother never knew who might visit or how long they might stay. At times she resented these impositions. She felt some took advantage of those who lived in Big Bend.

Julia said they had more company at their Burro Mesa ranch than they ever did anywhere else. Someone always came and they talked and shared stories about funny things that happened to them or to their friends.

Dr. W.E. (Bill) Lockhart, a special friend of my father's, came to Blue Creek deer hunting. He brought his friend Dr. Searls of Marfa. They hunted on horseback south and east of the ranch house. Dr. Lockhart called this the most remote part of the United States. He wound around in the hills all day with no luck finding deer. They became separated and Dr. Searls appeared lost. Bill told us later:

> I gave my horse "his head" not knowing where he would take me, but in any case almost surely to water, and I was thirsty. We came to a rock slide, and the horse stopped. I got down and led him over the slide. Sure enough, there would be the trail. After sunset and just before dark, we approached some vague buildings in the dusk. There was the Blue Creek ranch house, and I was home. But Dr. Searls stayed out all night. Next day he came in wild eyed and scared. "Why didn't you give your horse his head?" I asked. He replied "I didn't know but what Homer might have bought that horse in Mexico!"

My mother spoke of a similar experience. She wanted to go along head lighting for ringtail cats — smaller, raccoon-like animals with short fur like a beaver's. The pelts had a higher value than many other skins. Head lighting involved hunting at night by a light thrown from a lamp strapped to the top of your head. The light caused the animal's eyes to glow. She recalled the experience to me:

> Over there at Blue Creek, those hills are real high and rugged. At last Homer consented that I could go head lighting, and he had this fellow from Comstock who went along with us. His name was Brotherton — he worked for us. Well, we went and Homer gave me instructions. I'd go there and here'd be the trail again. You would look way down. When we got in those canyons of nothing but slick rock, I'd ride and think, "This looks a little dangerous with a shod horse." Of course, I didn't really know. I just went blithely along. Brownie took me over those bad places.
>
> Of course, Homer knew I was safe on Brownie, such a sure-footed horse. Homer rode a mule I think. He would pick the easiest. Well, I went along. It must have been midnight when we got back and we missed this fellow, Brotherton. We waited and waited for him, but he didn't come. He never did come, so we went to bed.
>
> The next morning he came up to the house. Homer said, "Where were you?" The man said he fell off one of those trails and right into a bunch of cactus. He rode a mule too, and they're supposed to be so surefooted. He picked out cactus and then he walked home, all because I wanted to go head lighting. They had it in for me because I always thought up something.
>
> The only thing about head lighting is Homer thought he was so smart and could tell by the eyes, and when he got over there, he shot one of his best sheep.

My father talked about opening parts of the ranch to paid hunters in 1936. This began with a group of four men from Dallas, Ft. Worth, and Wichita Falls — engineering friends from his college days. We needed another source of cash income at this time.

These men left Marathon early in the morning, arriving at Oak Springs at late noon. After a meal of venison, frijoles, cake and lots of other trimmings, they walked up the mountain side to test their rifles as to sight alignment and their nerves as to jitters. When they asked how the Chisos Mountains got their name, Daddy told them he thought the name came from the Spanish, meaning Ghost Mountains, suggested because of the filmy draperies of blue-gray clouds often shrouding their summits.

After this, they motored some five miles up Blue Creek Canyon through the dry creek bed in the narrow rock gorge with mountains and multi-colored rock cliffs towering above them on each side, looking as if to pierce the sky. After arriving at Javelina Pass, and scotching their car with rocks to prevent its voluntary escape down the canyon, they unpacked the camping and hunting equipment then turned the entire program over to the Mexican guide, cook and horse wrangler, Luna, who soon had the belongings packed down on the backs of sure-footed mountain ponies and mules. He told them they had some four or five miles to go further up into the mountains to the permanent camp in Cherry Springs Canyon.

At the pass, it seemed like they climbed straight up and had to hold on to keep from sliding backwards out of their saddles. Arriving at the top of the pass, they found themselves far above the swift-moving, low-hanging clouds that hurried by beneath them. Cold penetrated their jackets as they looked down the 3,000 feet into the canyon below. The descent on the other side appeared even more precipitous, so they decided to take it on foot and lead the horses. Luna, however, suggested, "Horse no fall," and they hurried down with no mishaps.

Homer Wilson, 1932.

Shearing pens one mile below Ward Springs.

Goat pen at Blue Creek.

Angora goats on a hill overlooking Oak Creek Canyon.

Sam and Nena Nail on the way to their ranch after their wedding.

The Sam Nail family home. Two miles west of the Wilson home at Oak Creek.

Camping near Cedar Springs.
Sam Nail on rock in center.

Simón Victorino with Hupmobile on the Wilson Ranch.

Bergine, Patricia, and Homer Jr., with mountain lion.

Hunting friends.

Hunters on cedar posts at the head of Blue Creek.
Homer on left.

Patricia at Cattail Falls.

Cattail Falls.

Rio Grande catfish.

Fish fry at the Rio Grande.

Lott Felts, foreman, roping deer with locked horns on the Wilson ranch.

Bergine with an eagle.

A trapped panther.

Patricia on her horse Walkalong.

Patricia and Thomas.

Chata's place at Boquillas.
Left to right: Carlos Cortez, Chinita, Doña Chata,
Don Juan Sada, and Guera or her small sister.

*Evelyn and Dorothy Burnam, Julia Nail, Homer Jr., Patricia,
and Fred Darge.*

*Homer Jr., Patricia, and friends
overlooking the Ranch at Oak Creek Canyon.*

Homer Jr., Patricia, and Thomas
with Bergine by the gate at Oak Creek.

Homer and Thomas at Blue Creek.

*Thanksgiving turkey and Patricia with
her .22 Long Rifle at Oak Creek in 1944.*

Here, and in other places in the Chisos area, most everything that grows bears a thorn. The devil's walking cane, the peculiar growth with eight to ten spike-lined prongs that waved back and forth in the breeze, seemed to lure the horses, perhaps for the curry comb effect on their sides, but much to the discomfort of the riders. Without care, a hunter might step in the middle of a bunch of lechuguilla, the low cactus growth whose darts penetrated boots at will.

They hunted from horseback, but dismounted before shooting, often resulting in a spill for the huntsman and the buck getting away. The deer slept high upon the mountainsides, often in the narrow gorges filled with rocks and brush undergrowth. The hunter approached such a position rather quietly, then dismounted, loosening huge boulders that tumbled down the mountainside, scaring the buck who then emerged from the gorge and ran up the other side of the mountain.

The hunters said their biggest thrill came from seeing this hitherto little known country. They saw huge cedars with weeping foliage that drooped in long streamers similar to weeping willows. Atop the summit of Emory Mountain they found themselves in a cold, heavily wooded forest containing pine and fir trees ranging seventy feet and more in height, manzanita bushes bearing large red berries on which the bears fed, and numerous other growths native to far northern climates. This phenomenon contrasted with the dry, cactus-covered foothills below.

* * * * *

Since my father seldom mentioned money problems or concerns about an approaching national park, I failed to understand the magnitude of these problems. I sensed something ominous looming in our future. Now and then Daddy frowned without reason, wiped his forehead, gazed in the distance, and hugged me a little closer than usual.

Mother didn't have this trait of shielding the children and

not sharing feelings with them. The Depression made it obvious that we had financial strains. Everyone did. No problem for us kids. We had what we needed in my thinking. Who wanted more than a beautiful place to live, a wonderful place to explore, and good neighbors as friends?

The approaching park seemed an enigma. Even Mother tended to show frustration by slamming pots on the stove, gritting her teeth, and looking grim. Our neighbors stopped talking when I entered the room, and Julia's smile grew softer and sometimes sad. In a sense the atmosphere felt like someone died. The loss of our land, like the loss of a dream, loomed before all of us in Big Bend.

Mother thought the many visitors coming in the early 1930s brought on the idea of a national park. She said they went home and raved about the unusual beauty of this area. My father seemed to believe the majority of people in west Texas thought a national park might bring tourists and money to the area. Julia told me she thought the hard times of the awful drought along with the bad times of the Depression made people "lose heart" and contributed to their willingness to accept the park idea. I didn't know what to believe except that I hated to lose our paradise.

Later, when I asked Mother about the possible national park, she said the whole thing sneaked up on us. In 1933 the State of Texas established a park called the Texas Canyons State Park using fifteen school sections owned by the state. They added lands given up for non-payment of taxes. Then, in 1935, Roosevelt signed a bill authorizing the establishment of Big Bend National Park, but the State of Texas had to get the land. In 1937 Governor James Allred vetoed a bill that would finance this. He said Texas didn't have the money needed. That's where we stood in 1940, the idea surrounding us like a low cloud of poisonous gas drifting our way and accelerating even without the needed funding.

Those of us who lived on and owned the land in this area loved it as home. We worried about giving up our homes and leaving this land. We cherished the desert, the mountains, and the vast spaces. The people had hardships in this rough country and isolation brought challenges peculiar to Big Bend. For the most part, they solved their conflicts with nature and treasured this life away from crowded cities. Generally, those who lived in Chisos country opposed the park idea, but felt themselves at the mercy of the government.

Chapter Fourteen

AN OPEN VISTA

My parents seemed happier in 1940. Prices improved on wool and mohair, good rains fell in the Chisos, and the mine produced more mercury. Mother smiled and laughed more, though she still worried about the park taking away our land, but said she wouldn't complain until she knew for sure the government would take our ranch. She shrugged then and read a favorite book. Sometimes she put one of the paper records with 1920s music on the old wind-up Victrola. The bouncy, joyous songs filled the porch and spilled into the front yard.

In 1938 my parents bought a little stucco house in town so Buzzy and I could go to school in Alpine. I had the best classmates and friends there, but missed living all of the time here at Oak Canyon.

When we returned for the summer, I found my horse, Walkalong, in the section-sized pasture at Oak Creek. After I bridled him and rode him bareback back to the shed, I saddled him and went for a ride up the trail toward the Window where I noticed the tall mountains, the deep canyon, and the simple things like the rock squirrel chattering at me from some boulders and the cactus wren with her nest in the cholla cactus, its thorny, pickle-shaped stems creating a spiny barrier to snakes and other predators. This wren reminded me of our lives here in this beautiful wilderness, surrounded by sharp rocks and dangers yet singing our love for our homes. Julia calls our situations poignant.

I thought about many things then. When I fed the chickens in the evening, I noticed the orange and black rooster strutting by the hens. They threw their orange heads up then ran as the corn hit the ground near the chicken house. Just before they reached the feed, they braked then pecked and scratched like they doubted the wealth of extra food. We also stopped at times, not sure that better times might stay with us. It seemed all of us wondered what waited for us beyond the next hill.

I heard happier stories now. Mother laughed as she told about her Bantam chickens when she first came to the Chisos:

> A friend gave me three Banty chickens. Their iridescent feathers and feisty personalities emphasized their small stature as they strutted and preened. They rode quietly in a cardboard box with holes poked in the sides and top. I carried them into our room at the Gage Hotel. At daylight the rooster crowed a rasping call, waking many hotel guests. Anyone but me would anticipate this happening! People had another laugh at my expense.

Her ability to laugh at herself endeared her to us and to many others who chuckled with amusement, not spite.

The Leona and Elberta peaches ripened the last part of July in 1940. A small ditch channeled cold water down from the spring, allowing irrigation for our garden and the two orchards. In the early morning while the Chisos looked a misty blue and the sun caught droplets on spider webs, turning them to strings of jewels, the icy water poured from row to row, then tree to tree. In the cool of the morning we picked bushels of the luscious golden-red fruits. Buzzy and I clamored up the larger branches, taking the ripe peaches for our smaller buckets. As we sampled our wares, sweet juices ringed our mouths and chins.

Mother insisted my brother and I each peel a bushel of peaches before we went out to play. We sat on the edge of a bed on the front porch for this job. Curls of skin dropped from the apple peeler, then we plopped the sticky peaches into a tub of water so the outer covering did not darken in the air before Mother sliced and processed the fruit.

She canned in glass jars then placed these containers of sliced, pickled, and preserved peaches on shelves lined with newspaper in the pantry off the back porch. Once, while she canned on the wood stove, the pressure cooker blew up and sprayed fruit on the kitchen walls where hot juices and chunks ran down the wallpaper. Our luck held that time as all of us were sorting and scraping on the porch when the explosion sounded.

This year, Mother decided to try drying our harvest. We needed to do something more than share with friends and can what we couldn't eat. After peeling a large pan full, I carried the heaping slices out the upstairs hall window onto the back porch roof. Here I spread the thin, juicy segments on clean, cloth sheets. The bright, hot sun began to dry them when thunder rumbled to the southwest. Before I rescued our slices, a downpour came causing our peach-drying experiment to fail. After that, Mother reverted to canning again. Even when nature brought failure, we had another chance to win or a way to alter our direction and succeed.

That thought nagged at the back of my mind. The park problem differed from the rain spoiling the peaches. With the park, we might lose everything. Like Mother said, though, we must live in the present, not the past or future. We couldn't do anything about the park but wait.

* * * * *

Ranch life went on as usual the summer of 1940. Added to the regular activities of riding fence, tending water supplies, predator control, and screwworm checks, we faced the large jobs of rounding up stock and shearing in August. The main difference that year came when I took part in more of these chores. I was thrilled to go along and felt that I helped.

Buzzy and I needed to ride our horses to Blue Creek if we planned to participate in any major ranch activities. When we arrived there, added part-time men had thrown their saddles over the hitching rail outside the gate. Extra horses milled in the trap east of the yard, and excitement filled the air. Sheep filled the enclosures and dust swirled. The pungent smell of sheep manure lingered near the pens. Tomorrow, workmen planned to move these animals over the hills to the pasture below Ward Spring near the shearing pens.

I helped with the gathering of stock, but Homer Jr. stayed at the house, although he might help herd sheep later or pull mohair from the cat claw brush when the Angoras became entangled. We all got up before daylight. By the time I put on my blue jeans and long-sleeved shirt, Mrs. Felts and Mother had breakfast ready. Slab bacon popped and sizzled in a big, iron skillet. I smelled scrambled eggs warming and hot biscuits baking with the aroma of frijole beans, always ready for any meal, even breakfast.

The first thing that morning I brought in the horses from the half-section, fenced-in trap. If not careful in the dark, I could stumble on rocks or step on a cactus. Excited and determined to do this job well, I hunted the horses by sound as their shod hooves clinked on the stones. When they threw their heads up, they looked like paper silhouettes against the pale colors of the breaking dawn. After I drove them to the pens, we each bridled and saddled our own horse.

Three workers and I rounded the trail below Signal Peak

to gather the sheep from the pasture to the south. We turned east past the mountain while four other hands rode south. All of us wore hats with wide brims to shield us from the hot sun. The workers wore chaps to protect their legs from thorns and brush.

Moving sheep appeared easy after we found them. However, since they rarely stayed in large groups, finding and gathering them became a tedious process. Also, even though our sure-footed horses and mules seldom stumbled or fell and could travel most of the mountain country, climbing among rocks and boulders slowed our progress. As the sun soared above us, the sheep began to curl up under overhangs and under brush making them less visible. Also, they often fed among the crags and summits of the highest peaks and must be chased down into the foothills. My job included watching the sheep already gathered while the men clamored up the mountainsides and pursued the stragglers. Heat shimmered on the horizon looking in places like waves of water, a mirage that fooled the eye. The milling sheep stirred the dirt and sand in the arroyo as we crossed, sending puffs of dust around the animals. The smells of wool and sweat floated with the waxy odor of greasewood and cropped grass.

We gathered the sheep then drove them back to the pens at Blue Creek. The next day we moved these animals over the hills to the shearing pens two miles north of Blue Creek where several thousand animals awaited shearing. Only a small number fit in the pen by the shearing truck. Dust from the milling animals whirled and blew at our faces. I pulled my red bandana over my nose to lessen the dirt, but found this didn't help much. The hot August sun beat down on herders and animals.

The gathering, herding, and shearing of the sheep and goats took several weeks. This became quite an achievement since the crew clipped 4,824 animals in 1932, 6,008 in 1933, and 8,108 in 1934. I heard Daddy say he expected to shear nearly 6,000 this year.

It took Mr. Felts and twenty-three men handling the moving of sheep to and from the pens at Double Mills, as Mother called the shearing pens. Daddy stayed near the loading rack, numbering and identifying the bags of wool and mohair before workers stacked them for Mr. Wedin who hauled them to the train in Marathon. From there the bags went to the wool house in Del Rio for weighing, sale, and then crediting to the Wilson account.

The visiting crew erected tents for sleeping and eating some distance from the enclosures. During the day, they worked under a large tent with the shearing truck. A gasoline motor ran the six or eight metal arms, equipped with clippers. The gasoline motor rasped and chugged, clippers whirred, animals bleated in protest, and men shouted orders as work progressed, filling the open-air tent with a mixture of harsh and rough sounds and pungent odors of gas and manure.

Each clipper worked at his individual station on a wooden platform. An assistant did odd jobs such as bringing disinfectant when a clipper nicked an animal or carrying a fleece to a table for classing. From there, he delivered the mound of cream-colored wool to a wooden framed tower where he dumped it into a suspended burlap bag.

Here a presser stomped the fleece, pressing it until another bundle fell into the bag where the stepping continued until the bag filled. I begged to press the wool, and once in a while the man smiled and let me climb the frame and jump up and down on the fleece. The oily and sweet smell of lanolin with the bitter odor of burlap and the strong scent of sweat drifted from the rack.

Finally, the worker released the bag from the frame and sewed it shut with rough string, leaving ears at the bag's ends for easier loading. The assistant heaved the filled bag onto the pile of sacks that awaited hauling in Mr. Wedin's flatbed truck.

After shearing the animals each day, we drove the sheep and goats back to the hills as soon as possible for cover in brush and caves. Otherwise, they might die from exposure without their coats. This happened to a man on the other side of the mountains. He left his 2,000 goats in pens after shearing, and they died when it rained that night.

Mr. Nail, a successful cattle rancher, bought some goats as a one-time experiment. When it stormed, my father knew Sam just sheared those goats, so Daddy rushed to tell his friend to move the animals to cover. However, Mr. Nail had already driven the shorn goats up Burro Mesa to shelter. My father feared his friend might lose all of his new animals.

Shearing time meant having strangers on the ranch. It also brought neighbors who came to cut out any of their livestock that got onto our land in the past six months. The Babbs came from the southeast side of the Chisos to look for missing stock. I saw Boye Babb and his son, W. L., riding toward me wearing black hats, looking like men out of a western movie. During shearing they stayed at the Blue Creek house with us. We children loved this excitement. I don't know how Mother and Mrs. Felts liked the extra people living and eating in the house. If it bothered them, they did not complain.

Boye Babb, with W.L., Smokey, and Mildred Babb Adams and her husband, all lived on Boye's land. Apache Adams remembered a story about his parents living above the rim where Babb's land bordered ours. Mildred and Ulice stayed in a little rock house about a half mile from the South Rim. One day Apache's father decided to ride down the Blue Creek Canyon trail to our headquarters at shearing time. That trail had treacherous switchbacks and steep slopes. Soon their horses came to and stopped by a maguey pole leaning across the path. Finally, they jumped over the wooden bar and walked on down the narrow, rocky track. Not far down the trail, another maguey stick leaned across the trail. The horses stopped again and then vaulted over the dead stalk.

When Mr. Adams reached the Blue Creek headquarters some five miles to the southwest, Daddy asked him, "How did you get here?" He squinted, then narrowed his brows.

"Came down that Blue Creek Canyon trail." Mr. Adams smiled and wiped his brow of sweat. His spurs clinked as he walked to tie his horse at the hitching post.

My father swallowed and frowned. "Did you see those maguey stalks across the path?"

"Yes, but our horses stopped, then jumped over them."

"That's how I set a panther trap. I place it in a trail, then lean a maguey or sotol stalk across the path to warn people there's a device to catch a mountain lion."

Other unusual things happened when we sheared. I remember Mother grumbled when a man came to stay at Blue Creek at shearing time once. She said his socks stood by themselves by the bed. I didn't see or smell them, but believed what she said. His neck looked like it needed a little soap and water too.

While the crew worked, the women and sometimes the younger children spent time in their large tent making exquisite, colorful paper flowers. They cut, twisted, and wired these creations while the men sheared. Julia told me a young man who worked for the Nails also made bright, colored paper roses in his spare time.

My vivid memories of creative crafts came from watching other Mexican workers make beautiful things out of common materials. One man at Oak Creek took wire from our small, open dump. He twisted and straightened these old strands into doll furniture for his daughter. I saw the elaborate backs to these tiny pieces fashioned from leftover metal threads. Another ranch hand made eye-catching wall ornaments of cut metal from discarded tin cans. One of his fascinating decorations looked like a bird in a flowering tree.

* * * * *

My father and Harris Smith increased production again at their Fresno Mine. The operation included sixteen claims with a cinnabar ore reduction plant and furnace. Work at this time in 1940 involved the flotation process where the workers dug, ground, and mixed water with the ore-carrying rock. Cinnabar, heavier than other stone materials surrounding it, sank to the lowest level of the mix. After this concentrated bottom material dried and the chunks were fired, liquid mercury ran free to be bottled in iron flasks for shipment.

By 1939, when work began with homemade equipment, only a few flasks filled. They used well casings for retorts, vessels used to heat the ore for smelting. My father's geological exploration found new and larger deposits of cinnabar enabling expanded production. Funds proved a problem, but my father borrowed money from relatives, and Mr. Smith sold his Angora goats to finance increased labor expenses and purchase a large, rotary furnace. Production grew.

On our many trips to Fresno, I spent much time exploring the fossil-covered hills or wading in Fresno Creek. Two incidents stand out in my mind. First, Daddy let me go down in the shaft in a bucket. The dark, cool stone and dirt shadowed my descent. I feared the bucket might tip and dump me to the bottom of the hole. As the rope lowered, I was thrilled to see the layered rocks and stones. At the bottom, light from a lamp sparkled off some shards on the tunnel floor. This cinnabar deposit had a crystalline factor, making it different from many other area deposits.

Another memory from those early mining days involved my putting several pennies in an open iron pot holding a few inches of liquid mercury. I heard mercury turned copper to silver and hoped to experiment. This infuriated my father. "What in the world do you think you're doing, Patricia? Don't you know you can poison yourself by touching quicksilver? You might lose all of your teeth like Harris did. Never touch mercury! Never!" Tiny beads of sweat lined his graying, receding hairline as he leaned toward me. His blue eyes narrowed and the corners of his mouth tightened.

My head dropped, and I cringed. "I won't, Daddy. Never.

I promise." It seemed terrible to disappoint him. He seldom scolded me, and I wanted to keep things that way.

Most of the time, my father shared fun things about science and geology in the Big Bend. He told me interesting information about this section of the country, pointing out many geological phenomena during our trips. He told me the Chisos Mountains and the surrounding uplift formed millions of years ago. He compared this to the earth suffering from indigestion and throwing up molten lava that raised the entire area. The magma broke through the ground's surface forming intrusions at the top of the uplift. When these cooled, they became formations of reddish mountains. Later plateaus formed with deep chasms and gorges from erosion.

Once, as we sat on some rocks above Blue Creek, Daddy showed me how to tell how far away rain might be by measuring the time between a flash of lightening in the distance and the subsequent thunder. We watched thunderheads miles to the south. In that country, sheets of rain dragged below the dark undersides of clouds, dropping life-saving moisture on some places then missing others in an unpredictable manner, like a mother who favors one child over another. The landscape looked like a patchwork quilt with swatches of sunlight striking the desert by gray, shadowed areas near blue mountains in the distance, complimenting the reds of the cliffs of the Chisos.

This brief time in 1940 reminded me of the resurrection plant, a three- to six-inch, fern-like cluster of gray-green leaves that curled into a ball of dried, brownish, dead-looking matter. When watered, though, it opened and greened in a short time, a miracle to me.

Our improved times made me feel our lives altered with any new blessings, like the resurrection plants greening and opening with a summer shower.

Chapter Fifteen

LIGHTNING FLASHES

My father invited Dr. W. D. Lockhart and his wife, Lora Bell, to Blue Creek to go hunting. That cold, gray day of December 6, 1941 lives in my memory. Dr. Lockhart wrote about this experience:

> I shot a spike buck hunting on foot up Blue Creek from the ranch house. Lora Bell carried the gun back as I packed the dressed deer. Toward evening — it was cool — I hung the deer up under a platform some 150 feet southeast of the porch, and Homer went down to look at it. As he stood there he had a serious heart attack and all but died!
>
> Although he appeared older than his years with some gray hair in his forties — with a young, enthusiastic, pretty wife and two young children (Tommy was not yet hatched) — he had been a vigorous, active man prospecting all over the Big Bend for mercury, etc. He was educated as an engineer, and was a very intelligent, alert man. He was

an upright and honorable man. When other men had a dispute, not rarely they would go to Homer, for he was much respected.

There was some doubt as to whether I should be hunting deer in Blue Creek, but I was Ray William's, Ross Maxwell's, and George Shelly's doctor, so Bergine insisted that we come.

Luckily, I had my bag with me with morphine and atropine for Homer's major coronary thrombosis, which left him an invalid for his remaining two to three years. At that time he was heavily in debt having bought his ranch. Spared from death in the heart attack, Homer later lay in bed at home in Alpine and directed the Fresno Mine with Harris Smith's collaboration. This mine produced approximately ten percent of the U.S. mercury during World War II. I used to tell Homer every tenth tracer bullet was his.

We waited to bring Homer to Alpine, and in the morning Bergine, up getting breakfast and listening to the radio, broke the startling news: "The Japanese have attacked Pearl Harbor!"

Mother's story of this crisis varied from Dr. Lockhart's:

Homer walked down to that brush arbor to see the deer Bill hung there. Homer said, "Well, I hope you didn't shoot it in the ham." Just then he collapsed. Luckily, Bill had his bag in his parked car so he could treat your father. We got him into a bed. I was two months pregnant with Tommy at the time. Bill said we couldn't move Homer.

I have a vivid memory of this time also. Mother sent Homer Jr. and me out to remove Angora goats from the cat-claw brush. We rode our horses over the sotol-covered hills west of the house. From the tops of the ridges, we looked to the bottoms of gullies for a white puff like a cotton ball in the dark green bushes, a sign a goat's long hair held in the curved thorns. We then rode down and loosened the mohair, freeing the animal. Now that I look back on that time, I realize she found work for us so we wouldn't bother her as my father hovered near death.

Mother slept on a cot by my father's bed. He called to her.

"Bergine, I want you to take me to town."

"In the middle of the night?"

"Yes. I want to get a lawyer."

"I hate to think of doing that, Homer. Do you feel that you're going to die?"

"This fibrillation has been going on for two hours. I just hated to tell you."

"If you really feel that way and you're willing to turn it over to me, then I'm going to do what I think is best."

So, she called a worker and they put one of those rubber mattresses in what mother called her beautiful car — a sport Chrysler with a wide back seat. They placed the suitcases between the seats and then the mattress. My father lay with his head to the right so he could see and talk to her. My brother and I sat in front.

Mother hurried over that terrible, rocky road to Marathon and then to Alpine as Daddy said to her, "Aren't you driving too fast?"

"No. Does it feel that way?"

"It feels like you're driving too fast."

"Oh, I don't think so, Homer. You just sit tight." Mother glanced at Daddy and smiled then gripped the wheel with both hands. I knew she worried when she wore that determined, little frozen look.

We arrived at Alpine between five and six in the morning. Mother hurried from the car and ran in to call Dr. Lockhart. A strong wind whipped the weeping willow strands by the stucco house. Buzzy and I shivered and followed her.

Mother said Dr. Lockhart seemed very upset. He told her, "You mean to tell me that you got him into town and he's still alive?"

"I sure did." Mother leaned against the dining room wall, clutching the black phone. Buzzy and I stood mute, not knowing what to say or do.

I heard the doctor's voice from the receiver, "Well, don't you dare touch him. Don't you move him at all. Leave him right in that car!"

He came over in his pajamas. "I can't believe my eyes. Homer is so far gone."

I didn't know what that meant, but could tell from the doctor's frantic actions that this situation must be desperate. I hung back, trying not to get in the way, but wanting to know what happened.

Dr. Lockhart said he knew the minute he looked at Daddy what happened. Strep throat. The heart enlargement showed plainly when the doctor X-rayed my father. In those days they didn't have penicillin, so his heart just sluffed off. He didn't think Daddy could live but a few hours.

Mother fixed that front bedroom like a hospital room and hired around-the-clock nurses. Two large oxygen tanks stood by the metal hospital bed. Smells of alcohol lingered in the hall with the sounds of hushed voices and the occasional whang of the metal bed crank or the hiss of oxygen. My father hovered near death for over six months at our house in Alpine. During that time, Dr. Lockhart treated him while consulting daily with heart specialists Dr. Hermann of Houston, Dr. Kopetsky of San Antonio, and Dr. Scott of Cleveland. My father's weight and electrocardiogram results in consultation with these doctors determined the doses of medication for that day.

Buzzy seemed very quiet during those times. I cared about him as well as Mother and Daddy, but I couldn't do much to help.

As the crisis passed, my father directed some ranch business from his bed in Alpine. He dictated letters to Mother, and she typed and mailed the correspondence. I knew Daddy worried about his situation, though, when I heard my parents talking in early 1942.

"Bergine, I don't know how Lott can manage without me at shearing. I've always been there to tell him what to do. If it's not handled just right, we'll have one big mess and a lot of dead animals. I always made decisions as we went along based on bad weather. Things like that."

"He'll just have to manage. You tell him the best you can. That's all you can do. What things can go wrong? Tell me, and I'll write to him."

"He might mix up those old woolsacks with mohair in them around the pen. He shouldn't put wool in them. It affects the price."

"What else?"

"The old ewes in the Mill Pasture need to be sheared first and put in the Burro Mountain Pasture until after shearing and then put half of them in the Big Trap or Cattail Trap at Oak. If he has enough men, he might send those over to Oak as soon as he shears them, picking out the heaviest ewes for that pasture.

"He'll understand if you tell him, Homer. Anything else?"

"Well, I always had a man at Oak get up the bucks in Cattail about the time I was ready to finish shearing the sheep and bring them over so the bucks could be sheared with the sheep and registered goats could also be sheared and sent back with the sheared bucks. He should just shear the sheep out of Ward into the Mill Pasture as he comes to them.

Mother took notes in shorthand, looking up as she finished. The writing looked like squiggles and dots to me.

Daddy sighed and turned his head on the pillow. "The short wool needs numbering as well as the long wool. The mohair and the kid hair need to be numbered beginning at #1 for each. If he doesn't have a board for writing and doesn't jot down the number of the last sack marked, he will make a mistake in spite of everything."

"Is that all, Homer?" Mother's voice sounded strained.

"I always put down in a small book the number of each

load Frank (Wedin) brought with the number of sacks of wool and mohair in each load. I went to all these precautions in the past and still had plenty of problems."

"Let me read this back to you to be sure I have it right." She didn't know much about the ranch and struggled to understand this kind of talk.

"Before that, Bergine, there's more. Someone must look at the tinaja below the windmill and fill the opening with brush and keep watch over the dry tank in the Mill Pasture. When they get through shearing, someone needs to loose herd the goats in the corner of Ward while others work the sheep. The pregnant ewes go in the big pasture and the muttons and all lambs go back in Ward as I'm selling some of them. Some lambs will need long tails cut and dabbed with tecole or they will get worms as it's been too hot. Then, Lott needs to put the pregnant nannies plus the old nannies in the Big Pasture. Leave any old reprobate mutton goats in the Mill Pasture."

Mother's face had worry lines by her eyes. She claimed the dry air and blowing wind caused wrinkles, but I felt she grew lines as she worried about Daddy.

"Bergine, tell Lott he'll just have to put the other goats at the head of Blue Creek in that small pasture we built. It would get cold enough and be mighty risky business to have them up there, but I don't suppose there is much feed on Kit Mountain. We always had so much trouble with them down there."

"I think I have what you want, Homer."

"Lott should count the salt on hand and let Frank bring enough to make a total of 150 sacks."

"I'll type what's jotted down into a letter, Homer. Don't fret. Lott will know what you mean and want. He's a good man. We're so lucky to have him."

Mother finished the letter to Mr. Felts. She looked tired as her fingers clicked on the keys of her Royal. While she worked, I wandered in to talk to Daddy. In my mind I wanted to tell him I could handle things at the ranch. Mother could take me to the Chisos and I'd tell Mr. Felts what to do. The irony of this passed by me.

However, I did notice and remember happenings and conversations. Although active mentally, physically my father continued as a near invalid through the spring of 1942. Any unusual stress might kill him. With this in mind, Mother did not tell my father about her labor in May of 1942. Instead, she drove herself in the middle of the night to Dr. Lockhart's office where she gave birth to my youngest brother, Thomas.

Summer approached, and Daddy wanted to go to the ranch and to the mine above Lajitas. So, my parents bought the first Nash automobile in Alpine. This car allowed the back seat to be made into a bed. Mother drove, Daddy rested on the mattress, and Tommy lay on the font seat with a pillow as a prop for his bottle. Sometimes Buzzy and I went too. Other times we stayed with our Aunt Gladys, Mother's sister, who came with her son, Noel, to help us in this critical time.

As my father's health improved, he walked and sat with people, visiting about ranch and mine affairs. He also talked with neighbors concerning the approaching park. His view seemed to be a fatalistic one. The government and most of the people in west Texas wanted the national park. If we didn't sell, they would take it with eminent domain. Therefore, we should try to get the best price possible and cooperate.

Our situation developed somewhat better as far as price for our place than some rancher's, as the State gave compensation for improvements made. My father had as much in fencing, water tanks, and buildings as he had in the land. Now that the State appropriated money for purchase of land for a national park, and a lawsuit found this use of funds legal, pressure increased for landowners to sell to the State.

Feelings also ran high with our neighbors. Though some absentee owners welcomed selling their land, most landholders hesitated and resisted selling to the State. Those who lived on and owned their land came to love it as home. We cared for the desert, the mountains, and this special way of life. We felt violated and did not want to give up and relocate.

Some thought tourists might trample the area and destroy the landscape. The owners knew the meager water supplies couldn't support large numbers of visitors. However, the Park people reassured the landowners they would take good care of the owner's holdings. The residents believed this and thought about sharing the beauty with others.

Our closest neighbors had strong feelings. Dorothy Burnam, who had lived at Oak Canyon in the past, felt that the wilderness and beauty would be ruined with tourists who didn't care about the country. Julia said the ranchers at first had sympathetic feelings to the park movement, but later, when forced to sell, they felt differently. She said it was a very sad time for all of us. A former neighbor's wife felt they had not been treated fairly or paid enough for their place. Our neighbors twelve miles to the northeast agonized about losing their land. She argued that losing their ranch took their son's heritage. The Burnhams' son fought in the war overseas at that time. Mrs. Burnham even wrote to President Roosevelt to please not take their land. The Wayne Cartledge family refused to sell their holdings. Wayne and Josephine Cartledge leased land to us on the south and southwest. At this time, Wayne ran cattle on his ranch near Castolon. He also owned, with H.E. Perry, the abandoned cavalry post and farm acreage on the Rio Grande. They established a trading post, post office, school, and a successful irrigated farming business where they raised vegetables, wheat, feed for stock, and cotton that they ginned at Castolon. Years after the Big Bend National Park came into existence, the store, La Harmonia, continued to operate. Wayne would not sell any of his holdings to the State for the Park. He continued to keep his land, waiting for an agreement to a higher price per acre. Finally, Wayne and his son, Gene, did sell their ranch land to the Park, but retained their acreage at Castolon. After this, Wayne operated the store for several years before selling it and the farm to the Federal Government. This delay in selling La Harmonia meant the historic Cavalry Post buildings remained untouched during the time when the Park administration pursued a policy of removing all signs of human habitation from the Park.

* * * * *

During World War II, ranchers had the same problems as others with many shortages of goods. The rationing of gasoline and tires proved a major issue with the isolated nature of Big Bend. This meant the owners must do more paperwork to apply for these items for themselves and their workers. Great distances required greater allowances for travel.

Daddy also worried about labor. Many young men left for the service, while some Mexican men went back to Mexico to avoid the draft, making fewer workers available for ranches and mines. Getting help became more and more difficult for remote ranchers. My father's solution came with hiring bonded men from Mexico.

Before the war years, ranchers hired occasional workers from the other side of the Rio Grande. During the war years, however, hiring aliens became unacceptable. America needed to know what foreign persons came into our country and where they stayed. To hire someone from Mexico during the War meant writing an application requesting a certain number of workers for a specific reason. A required bond had to be included with this request to our government. Once during this time, my father brought three workers from Chihuahua, Mexico, and the bond for these three workers came to $1,000. When workers returned to Mexico, my father's bonds would be returned.

These times for us seemed like the approach of a storm at

night. As the air grew charged with electricity, lightning flashed, revealing a brief glimpse of treacherous times. From the Window, the once pristine view had now darkened, obscuring the vista of our saddening and struggling lives.

PART III
END OF AN ERA

Few but the strong shall feel
with leathered hands
the tethered bands,
the weight and arc of Hawk.

Few but the true and blest
can dance to an inner song
and share with bird and beast
the Earth, the Feast.

From "Brothers"
Kitty McCord Mendenhall

Chapter Sixteen

THUNDER ON THE HORIZON

As my father's health continued to improve, so did production at the Fresno Mine. When a Mexican laborer found the first signs of workable cinnabar, Harris Smith came to Daddy and said, "You be the brains, Homer, and I'll be the brawn." They became full partners at that time with my father owning half of the land and contributing half of the expenses. Daddy's difficult geological mapping and exploration ensured new ore finds, one of them referred to as "huge."

The stresses of signing to sell our land for the national park added complications in production at the mine, and the continuing work of running a ranch in a remote wilderness showed on my father. Always tall and slender, he lost weight and vitality. His steps slowed and his face often looked tired and gray. More creases formed at the corners of his eyes, not laugh lines as Mother with a teasing voice used to call them. He often said, "I'm just exhausted, Bergine. I can't even think about the park. Maybe later after I rest."

Mother responded with nervousness and worried looks.

"Don't mind me. I'm just worried, Homer. I wish they would get the whole thing over with, and we could go on with our lives."

I watched them both when I was not taking care of my new little brother. He still wore diapers, but toddled barefoot where Buzzy and I played.

Daddy did sign the contract for the sale of the Wilson ranch to the State Park Board on May 25, 1942. Later he furnished Robert Cartledge, who represented the Texas State Park Board, abstracts to surveys of land he owned in Brewster County, Texas. All of this was within the Park area and came to a total of 1,222 pages. This ended our struggle to keep our land, though payment did not come at this time. Of course the agony of losing our ranch did not end then or later.

To relieve some of the stress for Mother, with a small child to care for, and my father, who needed transportation help, John Larsh, a sixteen-year-old son of Daddy's good friend, Poe Larsh, came to live with us during the summer of 1943. John was to learn about ranching and act as a driver. He reminded me of one of our bantam roosters, confident and tough-acting toward me, he thought he knew more about ranching than most young people, often lecturing me on the subject. I hated this. He wavered between being interested in playing with Buzzy and me, and thinking himself old enough for adult activities.

In a desert country of cactus and dry arroyos, water drew young people like all desert creatures. Buzzy and I spent much time wading in Oak Creek, making pools larger and deeper by building dams. We spent hours shoveling gravel and filling holes with dirt to stop the flow. We dug, stacked rocks, and backed-up a pool at least two feet deep in places. This particular dam exceeded our hopes. When the creek water settled, John came to see why we looked proud as we waded and splashed. The clear, cold water felt delicious on this hot summer day.

John appeared older, but he let his younger thinking

show that day. His deliberate step in the narrow part of the heaped gravel caused the dam to break and the water gushed through, taking dirt and gravel with it and ruining our extensive project. I glared at him. "You didn't have to do that!" I yelled. He laughed and walked away, leaving me seething.

I waited for my revenge. The next day, John went to the pens to treat the buck sheep with tecole. He strode with head high under his too-big cowboy hat, ignoring me. I sat on the top rail of the wooden gate and mumbled, "You better look out for those bucks, John!"

Of course he paid little attention and turned his back on the brutes, as expected. I said nothing more, but watched. As a ram lowered his curved horns, I called, "They're dangerous. You better pay attention like I say."

He ignored me again. Just then the buck charged across the thick carpet of dried sheep manure that muffled the sound of running hooves. Wham! The big ram hit him below his belt, knocking John to the ground. I had my vengeance.

A few days after this, on July 11, 1943, John drove my father to Presidio on an errand concerning the bonded men who worked for us. At that time, no "River Road" went from Terlingua through Lajitas to Presidio. The driver went to Marathon, through Alpine and Marfa, then on south to the port of entry where they stayed the night. They spent the next day with the immigration authorities before returning to our house late in the afternoon.

My father looked exhausted and hot as he stopped at the canvas bag by the screen door for a drink. I ran to him, hugged him, and remember his arm drawing me close. Then, he rested before dinner.

Daddy went to bed on the porch earlier than usual that night. He wanted a good night's rest, so he lay where a cool breeze passed over his bed. A coyote yipped toward Burnham's and the mournful call of an owl filled the air. Dark clouds passed over the mountains hiding the stars that night.

I awoke early the next morning as something flitted back and forth inside the screened porch where I slept on my cot. At first I thought it a bat, then realized a frantic bird was trying to escape. In order to catch the small winged creature and then release it, I leaped out of bed. It sailed back and forth, frequently hitting the screen. At last, it flew to the shelves built over the screening on one side of the porch and hid behind some rock specimens displayed there. Daddy's bed bordered this shelving. If I went outside, I might see the bird.

I slipped out of the door and crept beneath the salt cedar tree. As I gazed through the mesh in the soft morning light, I saw something wrong with Daddy. He lay in a peaceful manner on the bed, a sheet covering his bent legs. His half-open eyes glinted a hint of blue beneath his lashes. I shook my head and went inside to look again. Tears welled in my eyes as I saw his peaceful face, all signs of worry and tiredness erased.

Mother had to know. I trudged to her bedroom, where she lifted my little brother above her head as she lay in bed. They both laughed as she jiggled him, and he cooed.

"Mother, something's wrong." I hesitated and hung my head.

"What do you mean?" She flung her head and stared at me.

"On the porch. You need to look. It's Daddy."

She ran barefoot to his bed, braked like a frightened deer, then threw one arm over her face and leaned against the doorway to the dining room. "Oh, no! Oh, no! Oh, no!" Then she began to sob.

Mother went to Terlingua with John to radio Alpine for help while I took care of my brothers and stayed with Daddy. Hours later, an ambulance came to take my father's body to Alpine. Mother arranged for a funeral in Alpine and another graveside service at the Wilson family plot at the Masonic Cemetery in Del Rio. Our lives changed forever.

Una May Wedin (Narowetz), whose father hauled our

wool and livestock, wrote to me about my father's funeral in Alpine:

> The most eloquent and beautiful memory that I have regarding your father, Homer Wilson, took place in the vestibule of the church in Alpine just prior to your father's funeral.
>
> My father, Frank Wedin, dressed in a suit, white shirt and tie stood near the entry door into the church and I stood beside him.
>
> "You're sad aren't you, Daddy?" As I said this, a giant tear rolled down my father's cheek and he replied, "Yes, he was a prince of a man.," which says to me the high regard and love that Daddy had for your father.

* * * * *

At this time in July of 1943, Mother assumed full responsibility for closing the ranch before the deadline of December 31, 1944, when all residents agreed to leave. She applied and did get an extension of time because my father had died. This helped Mother very much.

In addition to shutting down the ranch, she took on some obligations concerning the Fresno Mine. The city girl who knew little about ranching and mining struggled to survive these obstacles. Often I found her sitting with her face in her hands. When I approached, she rallied. "Don't worry, Patricia. Your father always said to pick myself up and dust myself off and get back on if I fell off a horse. It just hurts."

Although Mother dealt with the Fresno Mine operation and the concerns and problems of running and closing down the ranch, she did not do this alone. Lott Felts, our foreman, continued to oversee ranch operations. Lott guided the business through the August shearing season with few changes in routine. His concern and help kept her courage from weakening.

Friends and neighbors advised Mother in many ways. They rallied behind her and gave her emotional support and counsel. Without these special friends, life would have been bleak. They enveloped her with loving concern, and we survived this dreadful time.

In the early days after my father's death, Mother filed papers requesting the release from the armed services of my cousin, Jack Ward, on a hardship disability. They granted this request in October of 1943. Mother then received a telegram from Amarillo saying Jack would soon be with us.

After Jack came, Mother and my two brothers went to Oak Creek for that first Thanksgiving without Daddy. Jack told her he would meet us at the house, but he wasn't there. Mother paced the floor in the kitchen. Wind blew willow branches against the side of the kitchen wall making a scraping sound. The fire crackled in the wood stove, sending out warmth and the smell of mesquite smoke. She gripped her arms across her chest and said, "Jack should be here by now. He promised."

"What's wrong, Mother?"

She gritted her teeth and grimaced, "We don't even have a turkey."

If nothing else happened, I could take care of that problem. Daddy always said, "If you have a problem, do something about it!"

Early the next morning, I put on my green wool coat and took my 22 Long Rifle Daddy had bought for me. I slipped out the screen door to hunt a turkey for Thanksgiving dinner. Since I had a good idea where one might be up the canyon, my concern focused on being careful and quiet. Sure enough, a gobbler ambled out of the shade of a large oak tree. Raising my rifle, I shot the bird in the head, then carried him by the neck to the house. Mother hugged me and praised my efforts. We had a fine dinner with Jack later that day. I didn't realize at that time that Mother's frustration covered her many worries. A turkey for dinner stood for these problems. I couldn't do anything about those other anxieties.

Having Jack to sell the livestock and begin closing the ranch did help. Mr. Felts also stayed with us for about three months after my cousin arrived. This gave Jack time to learn more about the layout of the different pastures and specific ways of managing the ranch work.

The final selling of livestock meant rounding up all of our animals and, as Jack said, "Toothing 'em out," or telling age by tooth condition. Two other cousins, Wally Hodge and Bill Ward, came from Del Rio to help age the stock before sale. Wally wore a reassuring smile, but Bill expressed concern.

"We have to have more workers, Jack." Bill waved his hands toward the milling animals. Tall and thin with chiseled features, he fit the cowboy type with his khaki pants and dusty boots.

"That's all I could hire. It's next to impossible to get laborers now with the War."

Tall and lean like his older brother, Jack looked dusty and tired. "I've been down to the river, and we have the three bonded men from Mexico. I don't know what else I can do. We'll just have to do the work with what workers we've got."

The next morning, Bill looked up to see extra men walking down from the hills. "I couldn't believe my eyes. They came out of nowhere. Just arrived! I don't know where they came from or who told them. Damnedest thing!"

One of our Mexican workers must have flashed a message to Santa Helena, but none of the hands ever claimed credit. *Avisadores* didn't talk about their message system. My three cousins just offered thanks for the extra help and didn't worry about who sent the message or the home base of the laborers.

When the animals sold, I wanted to keep my horse. I assured Mother I could ride him the ninety-six miles through Study Butte to our house in Alpine. This seemed very simple to me. Why did she object so strenuously? She did, however, understand my sadness about leaving the ranch and had my brother's horse and Walkalong trucked to Alpine where each day I took the two horses out into the tall, waving grass of a vacant lot to let them feed.

We left Oak Creek for the last time in mid-afternoon. At the gate to Nail's land, two buzzards soared above us. One circled and landed on a fence post, raised his wings for airing his feathers and cocked his red, bald head as we passed. Curious, beady eyes seemed to glare at me.

We bumped down the road past the mailbox. I thought of the watermelons the Johnsons had left for us in times past and the many picnics we shared with them and other neighbors.

Then we turned right on the dirt highway heading for Marathon. I remembered Julia telling me how she and her parents used to go to town in their Model T Ford by a different route, by Slickrock, Smallpox, and Red Bluff to the old ore road from Terlingua to Marathon. The rough roads and steep hills made them stop often to scotch (put rocks behind the wheels so their car didn't back down the hill). I saw her in my mind jumping out with a rock in her hands. It seemed to me, I might never see Julia again.

In the past, Daddy didn't scotch when we went up a steep hill, just backed down the road and got a running start. Sometimes we succeeded. Other times, we tried again until the pickup made it to the top. That day in 1945, Mother had no problem at Todd Hill. She drove her Chrysler and it crept to the top at a steady pace.

More memories flooded my mind. I remembered Mr. and Mrs. Nail driving down the gravel road ahead of us on the way to Marathon. Sam always drove the same speed regardless of the road conditions. When he came to a dip, Nena bounced. From our pickup behind them, it looked like she hit the ceiling. Daddy and Mother laughed and waited for the next dip. Now, my father would never drive us again. Sam, Nena, and Julia might not bounce along these rough roads either. My heart ached.

I thought of others who lived in Big Bend leaving with sadness in their hearts. They too felt they had no choice in the matter. When the Park officials said the land would be preserved the way it was, these people believed them, but left with regret. None of them wanted to leave their homes in this beautiful place.

My thoughts returned to the present time as Mother stopped at the top of Todd Hill to look back at the Chisos Mountains. The late sun blazed orange on the cliffs of the Window above our old home. A strong wind blew mother's skirt and my blonde hair. She clutched her waist and held Tommy's hand. Buzzy stood with me. All of us gazed at our homeland. I felt like a lost orphan. My nine-year-old brother turned to Mother and said, "I'm not Buzzy Wilson any longer. Call me Homer from now on." And we did.

Mother looked again at the mountains, then turned to us and announced, "I never want to go back again. It's too sad for me. I want to remember our life in my heart, the way it was when we lived below the Window."

Mother kept her word. She never returned, but I knew I would come back to this paradise of my childhood some day.

Chapter Seventeen

THE WINDOW CRACKS

A way of life ended when we left Big Bend. During the Depression and World War II our friends and neighbors lived by the unwritten code called "The Law of the West." Some of these lesser customs seem inconsequential after sixty years, such as men always wearing a hat. When they entered a room, they removed their hats, but didn't place them on the table. We did not track in dirt. Asking how many acres a person had ranked with asking that individual's bank balance. Politeness dictated inquiring about a person's family, then discussing the weather. Men stood for a woman or elderly person. On entering a room, a person should go first to the oldest one in the room. We always left a gate the way we found it. Finally, men tipped their hats in respect on the street.

Other customs and values held more importance. Someone might pass and be hungry, so we left our doors unlocked. Women and the elderly received respect. We helped our neighbors. People did not count what they did. As a friend said, "It was written in their hearts."

The people of Big Bend unconsciously followed these practices based on courtesy. They cared for and trusted one another in a genuine manner.

When I returned to the Chisos as a young adult, I found many changes. The National Park officials promised the ranchers they would care for the land and preserve it. This was their intent, but differing Park policies caused many alterations during the late 1950s and early 1960s. I found electric lines on tall poles going up Oak Creek and an outsized tank covering the spring at Oak Canyon so it didn't flow down the streambed. A pipeline lay from the tank over the falls area at the Window. Another large pipeline went to Cattail Falls. A sign warning visitors that the water might be unsafe stood near the trail to the creek. That pure water also flowed to the Basin for the many tourists.

James Owens found many differences when he returned to Big Bend in the 1960s, years after the area became a National Park. He had spent much time photographing the mountains, the desert, and the people of his CCC camp years between 1934 and 1937. Saddened by the changes, he missed the vanished homes of early settlers. He found much of the wildlife gone. When he lived in the Basin, large herds of deer passed by the mountain cliffs. He found parts of Big Bend crowded with visitors, but realized that Nature would prevail over civilization.

Big Bend families who remembered the days before the Park became unhappy with the many alterations and with the apparent disregard for the feelings of former residents. As time passed, other changes occurred. Park leaders had any signs that people once lived on ranches removed, bulldozing houses, buildings, and water tanks, then taking out pipelines and fencing. These directives included attempting to dynamite the baths at Hot Springs. However, moving the Blue Creek headquarters house proved too difficult. Its thick stone and concrete walls saved it as an example of a ranch home for that time. Perhaps, caring for homes required funds the Park did not have. Maybe officials had a national policy of removing buildings from Park property.

Once my brother Homer visited the Park and talked with a ranger about a water shortage in Big Bend. The ranger expressed concern for the wild animals.

"Why don't you fix those header tanks that my father built?" Homer pointed toward the upper gullies on the mountain slopes.

"Oh, that would cost too much money," the ranger said as he shook his head.

"Well, sell the forty miles of fence you removed from the Wilson ranch and use the money to fix the headers then." A slight smile tugged at Homer's lips.

"But, we gave that fence away," replied the Park official.

I also visited with a park ranger in the summer of 1990 about my life on the Wilson ranch before the Big Bend National Park. I thought this interview would be a friendly one of interest in pioneer life of the area. This individual opened the interview by saying, "How do you respond to the accusation that the ranchers in Big Bend destroyed the land by overgrazing?"

Speechless, I struggled to answer. Thoughts flashed through my mind of my father using great care to alternate pastures and not overstock. He believed if he took care of the land, it would take care of him. I remembered Sam Nail talking about cleaning out his many springs to keep them running for his livestock and the local wildlife. When the Park came, officials bulldozed these grottos, causing many to quit producing water. My mind flooded with scenes of neighbors caring for their land and worrying about drought. The rancher who owned his land was the real conservationist. My father believed in careful use of natural resources. Other ranchers in the area felt the same way.

Dr. Clifford B. Casey, in a series of papers printed in 1969 by the U.S. Department of the Interior under the name, "Soldiers, Ranchers and Miners in the Big Bend," wrote:

The Oak Canyon–Blue Creek Ranch rarely found it

necessary to provide extra feed for the livestock. Wilson had an excellent range for raising sheep and goats, and his major problem was one of effectively using the range by judiciously tending his herds so that they derived the greatest possible benefit from the native vegetation. During a few of the dryer years he made some use of his own sotol plants; however, this was infrequent and of little consequence during the fifteen years of his operation of the ranch. This situation was assured by careful use of his range and a definite policy of not overstocking the ranch. As a matter of fact, on a number of occasions during the 1930s, he pastured livestock for neighboring ranchmen whose ranges were unable to carry their stock.

In looking back, I wondered if the weather might be a large factor in the decline of the range. Grasses and other forage seemed plentiful in pictures on the Wilson ranch in the 1930s and 1940s. Removing sources of water could force animals to leave Big Bend also. The large herds of deer vanished after the area became a National Park. Too many large predators for the number of prey might be another answer to declining numbers of wildlife in the Chisos area.

Ranchers received much criticism because they attempted to control predators that killed their livestock. One theory is that the Park's policy of protecting the large predators caused an imbalance in nature. Landowners as far north as Alpine found it difficult if not impossible to raise livestock since the panthers ranged more than seventy miles a night, hunting then returning to the protection of the Park. Some mountain lions have been sighted in the Alpine area; one crossed the back yard of a home there. Shy pumas became bolder with human association. Within recent times, a panther attacked a small boy as he walked with his parents on a Park trail. The animal mauled the child, chewed off the boy's scalp and swallowed it before the father grabbed a stick to beat the animal off the boy. This aggressive behavior by a mountain lion, unheard of in times before the Park, caused many persons to become wary of dangers from the large predators.

Other hazards lurked in Big Bend and continued to exist after the Park. Anyone lost in that country caused worry and panic. This rough area of sharp stones and boulders with cactus and poison-tipped plants such as the lechuguilla held dangerous snakes among the rocks and thickets. Even a scorpion or a centipede gave a painful sting. The lack of drinking water became a hazard and staying out in the hot sun without a hat caused sunstroke. Most of the time people who lived in Big Bend avoided trouble, but young children and untrained outsiders often risked disaster.

In the early years of the Park, a Houston couple pulled their station wagon into the old wagon road from Castolon that went to Blue Creek. The car stalled and refused to start again. The man stayed with the vehicle; the woman walked toward the Chisos Mountains for help. Ross Maxwell Drive did not exist at that time. The man died at the automobile from complications of exposure. The woman wandered until she found a seep spring. She did stay near this water source and sought shelter in a small cave. Air and ground search lasted about a week before they found the woman. Water and shelter saved her life.

Even with many differences today, some things remain the same in Big Bend. The land, still rough and unforgiving, holds dangers for visitors. The beauty of the mountains, canyons, and desert remain for many to enjoy. Housing development did not spread into this wilderness as it has in other places. For these I offer thanks.

Today, Park officials and volunteers express interest in the heritage of Big Bend. They now have interpretative programs designed to give the visitors an appreciation and understanding of the cultural history of the area before the Park. Many travelers express interest in the animals, birds, and plant life of Big Bend, but a large number of persons ask about the people who once lived in the area. These tourists want to know how people survived and lived in such an isolated place.

Management encourages programs that benefit both visitors and Park staff. One of these is the Pioneer Reunion that brings speakers to the Park headquarters to share stories of early Big Bend. Also, a majority of ranger programs today consider the cultural aspects of the Park. These efforts indicate a real interest by Park officials in saving the best of the past for the future enjoyment of the people who visit Big Bend.

One of the old oak trees still stands at Oak Canyon. It leans almost to the ground now. That tree is about all that is left of the home place on the Wilson ranch.

In my mind, I look back to a way of life before the Park. I can see myself with my dog standing on a flat boulder when I was only eleven, streaked hair straggling across my tanned forehead, a colt of a girl, leggy, and awkward. The rock sprawled on the hillside spewed there millions of years ago by one of the silent volcanoes of the wild Chisos Mountains country. Cactus and mesquite rested against its coolness as the hot Texas sun baked its crust.

This boulder was my special, secret place. I used to stand there in the evening and wait to see Daddy's pickup truck lurch over the rugged rocky road as it crossed the last pasture. The lava of the jagged mountains, as iron red as the sun, hung above the blue ridge of the next ranch, making a glowing reflection on the cliffs like a face warmed at a campfire.

As my father swung the truck down the hill to the old two-story house, he honked. The whine made Angora goats rise lazily to let him pass and then amble slowly down the clay and gravel incline to the pens by the creek. Then I jumped from the rock slab, leaped over cactus and thorn, vaulted the fence by the peach orchard, brushed past the willows by the spring, and ran under giant oaks, their leather leaves whispering in the warm breeze. My dog barked and I laughed as we passed the salt cedar tree by the rock wall that fronted the frame house.

Sixty years fade again. Now the house is gone and many of the trees scraggly. I stoop to find a weathered nail, all that is left of the home where I grew up. Placing it carefully in my pocket, I smile as I remember Mother saying, "You'll be sorry if you try to go home. Things are never quite the same as you remember them." I realize Big Bend is not the same, but I have my memories. The wild beauty of this country remains for future generations.

About the Author

Patricia Wilson Clothier spent the first fourteen years of her life on the Wilson ranch in Big Bend, Texas. In these years, she experienced the Big Bend as a backyard filled with cherished treasures and inspiring adventures. After the formation of the Big Bend National Park, Patricia and her family lived in Alpine, Texas, then moved to Del Rio, Texas, where she graduated from High School.

Patricia, an artist and teacher, now lives in Shawnee Mission, Kansas. She and her husband, Grant, built and operated a camp for disadvantaged children in the Missouri Ozarks. Although over a thousand miles away, Patricia returns to southwest Texas as often as possible to visit friends and family, and to renew her spirit in the beautiful land of her childhood.